Detail in Contemporary
Kitchen Design

Published in 2008 by
Laurence King Publishing Ltd
4th Floor
361–373 City Road
London
EC1V 1LR
United Kingdom
e-mail: enquiries@laurenceking.co.uk
www.laurenceking.co.uk

A catalogue record for this book is
available from the British Library.

ISBN: 978 1 85669 570 1

Designed by Hamish Muir
Illustrations by Advanced Illustrations
Limited
Picture Research by Sophia Gibb

Cover image:
Tetsuka House, Tokyo
© Edmund Sumner / VIEW

Printed in China

Virginia McLeod

Detail in Contemporary Kitchen Design

Laurence King
Publishing

Contents

Introduction

Increasingly in contemporary homes, the kitchen is the most important space in the house. No longer relegated, as in the early twentieth century, to an ancillary 'below stairs' location where the cooking would be undertaken in isolation, possibly by servants, the kitchen is now at the literal and emotional heart of the home, where one person can prepare, cook and clear away a meal in the company of their family and friends. The demise of the isolated kitchen is linked to the abandonment of the formal dining room which in many small family homes and apartments was an under-used and increasingly unnecessary room. For this reason, the combination kitchen / dining room has now become a place where chores other than cooking are done, where children play or do homework, and where adults spent a great deal of time both looking after their families and socializing.

The labour saving possibilities of the modern kitchen have been made possible by the standardization of kitchen cabinets that have been designed to hold almost everything a cook could possibly need, and innovations in cooking and preparation appliances, many of which are now extremely sophisticated machines. The greater standardization and integration of cabinetry and appliances has also made it possible to mix and match items from different manufacturers to create a truly personalized space.

Not surprisingly, in contemporary homes the kitchen is the room on which the most amount of money is spent and the most amount of detailed consideration given, both on the part of owners and architects. This is true of both the cosiest of apartments and the grandest of houses. *Detail in Contemporary Kitchen Design* includes a range of homes, both modest and extravagant, revealing that the current preoccupations in kitchen design are universal. In all cases, however – despite the commonality of cooking appliances, well thought-out planning and efficient placement of preparation and serving areas – this book illustrates that the kitchen still has enormous scope for personal expression.

The diverse kitchens shown here include Westarchitecture's Bavaria Road apartment (page 10), in which a simple and inexpensive kitchen using off-the-shelf carcasses combined with custom made countertops, transforms the living spaces of this compact loft. Elsewhere, no expense has been spared to create truly dramatic kitchens that are masterpieces of planning, design and functionality. For example, Tzannes Associates' Parsley Bay Residence (page 144) employs a single material (stainless steel) to maximum effect by using it for cabinets, doors, drawers, work surfaces and handles in a kitchen big enough to service large catered functions as well as daily family life. Johnny Grey's kitchen for the Threshing Barn (page 178) is a essay in materiality. Here, luxurious timber veneers, stone, steel and glass are combined to create a sculptural presence at the heart of this luxurious home.

While not intended as a practical manual, this book provides an invaluable insight into some of the most beautiful and functional kitchens created by architects and designers in recent years. All of the projects and case studies are presented with photographs, plans, elevations and sections to provide an understanding of how great kitchens are conceived, designed and built.

Notes

Imperial and Metric Measurements
Dimensions have been provided by the architects in metric and converted to imperial, except in case of projects in the US, where imperial dimensions have been converted to metric.

Terminology
An attempt has been made to standardize terminology to aid understanding across readerships, for example 'wood' is generally referred to as 'timber' and 'aluminum' as 'aluminium'. However materials or processes that are peculiar to a country, region or architectural practice that have no direct correspondence are presented in the original.

Floor Plans
Throughout the book, the following convention of hierarchy has been used – ground floor, first floor, second floor, and so on. In certain contexts, terms such as basement level or upper level have been used for clarity.

Scale
All floor plans, sections, elevations and construction details are presented at conventional architectural metric scales, typically 1:50, 1:20 or 1:10 as appropriate.

Case Studies

Bavaria Road
Apartment
London, England, UK

Westarchitecture was established in 2006 by Graham West. For this elegant refurbishment of a double height living space within a former Methodist chapel in North London, large areas of the existing ceiling were removed and a new timber mezzanine suspended from the roof.

The mezzanine has a solid balustrade which gives a sense of privacy and enclosure to the new sleeping area. The platform is accessed via a folded steel staircase. All services were replaced along with the relocation of a new kitchen and a poured resin floor incorporating underfloor heating.

The Bavaria Road apartment was the Wood Awards Small Project winner in 2006 and was shortlisted for the AJ Small Projects Awards in 2007.

Graham West
Project Architect
Westarchitecture

This kitchen forms part of the overall refurbishment of a double-height living space on the first floor of a former Methodist chapel in North London. The owner contacted me through a mutual friend just after he had bought the property and realized he didn't want to do all the work himself.

One half of the main space was opened up to the roof to allow for the insertion of a mezzanine sleeping space. Originally the kitchen was located on the other side of the main space where it felt isolated and out of scale due to the 3.8 metre (12 1/2 feet) high ceiling. The new kitchen is now located underneath the mezzanine where the soffit is 2.4 metres (7 4/5 feet) above floor level. Here the scale is much more comfortable, with the mezzanine providing a sense of enclosure and definition to the kitchen space. In effect, the insertion of the mezzanine floor generated two spaces – the bedroom above and the kitchen below. The kitchen island and preparation area has been orientated to face the living room and is positioned adjacent to the dining area. Now the owner can talk to his guests, watch television or just look out of the windows whilst working in the kitchen. The dining area also benefits from the sense of intimacy provided by the reduced ceiling height.

We opted to have no high-level cupboards to keep the kitchen physically and visually separated from everything above. The cupboards on the wall are set out from the far side of the chimney breast, leaving a space for the freestanding refrigerator which lines up with the edge of the mezzanine above – which again contributes to the notion that its underside encloses the kitchen space. All electrical fittings and smoke detectors are connected out of sight above the timber battens of the mezzanine soffit. The kitchen itself is predominantly constructed from 'off-the-shelf' components using Ikea carcasses and doors all purchased directly by the owner who worked to overall setting-out dimensions provided by us. All assembly and installation was carried out by the main contractor responsible for the overall refurbishment of the apartment.

The island unit was custom built from MDF to house the dishwasher, washing machine and sink. The worktops are all birch-faced plywood to match finishes used throughout the apartment. Two 19 millimetre (3/4 inch) thick ply sheets are laminated together to form a 38 millimetre (1 1/2 inch) thick surface which is finished with clear yacht varnish. The owner originally intended this to be a temporary option, intending at some stage in the future to replace them with Corian. However, the birch finish is extremely hard wearing and doesn't appear to have suffered any perceivable wear and tear over the past year.

I hope that the kitchen meets the client's expectations. It is a very straightforward solution housed in an ambitious reworking of his original apartment. During the course of the project we both got to know each other well and have since become friends sharing the occasional home match at the nearby Emirates football Stadium, so I suppose that says something.

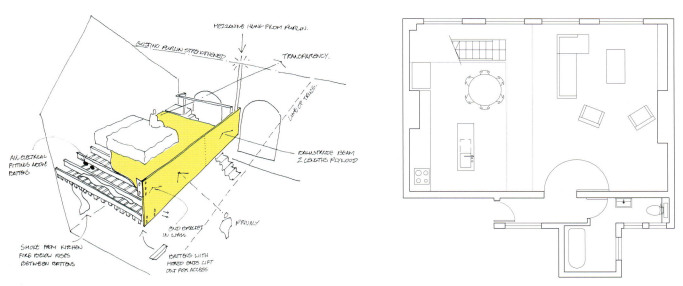

Above Left
Perspective sketch illustrating the apartment layout as well as elements of the structure. The mezzanine platform is the main organizing element in the space and provides an appropriately scaled space for the kitchen underneath.

Above Right
Floor plan. The apartment is essentially one open plan space, with the sleeping platform above the kitchen and a bathroom accessed via the entrance lobby.

Left
View of the kitchen from the living space. An elegant folded plate steel staircase rises up to the sleeping mezzanine with its birch-clad balustrade. The birch-ply kitchen worktops, used on both the run of wall units and the island bench, are the only deviation from the otherwise simple white colour scheme.

Henrik Sikstrom
Client
Bavaria Road Apartment

I always had the idea that when I got my own place, there would be a big brash industrial stainless steel kitchen. Having worked as a chef in my late teens, I was intrigued by what it would be like to have the rawness of something industrial in a domestic setting. I also thought that I would be able to put it together inexpensively by buying stainless steel units second hand from restaurant brokers or perhaps somewhere that had just gone out of business. But this was also during a time that I thought it would be great if the apartment resembled a turn of the century Parisian artist's studio. Let's just say that with hindsight, I'm extremely happy that a mutual friend introduced me to Graham West.

What was supposed to have started out as a small project to create a larger, more efficient mezzanine space than the existing one and perhaps do things up here and there in stages, grew into a full-scale overhaul of the entire apartment when I was seduced by Graham's plans and ideas. It was then agreed that it would be more convenient to address the entire renovation at once rather than in stages. At that point the kitchen was, in fact, the least of my priorities, as all I wanted was a larger bedroom area. However, the way the design was arranged, the kitchen naturally slotted in beneath the mezzanine, becoming almost an integrated part of it.

A great deal of the budget for the renovation was spent on 'invisible improvements' such as under floor heating, electrics and a new hot water system, amongst other necessary but perhaps not so exciting things, which meant that the kitchen had to be built with a very modest purse indeed. Since the building has no gas mains supply, I was determined to install an induction hob which I managed to source through ebay along with all the other appliances. With these, combined with carcasses from Ikea and worktops made by the contractor in plywood, I managed to achieve a result I was both able to afford and very pleased with.

My initial plan was for the kitchen to be a temporary solution, to be upgraded at a later stage, but I see no need for it now and I will be happy for it to stay like this for the foreseeable future.

There was a lot of hardship, stress and discomfort involved in the renovation of the apartment, but the good things far outweigh the negatives. Friendship and trust has been forged and I have already given the green light for Graham's new plans for another loft extension which incorporates another extraordinary staircase. I suppose home improvements are a bit like tattoos, quite moreish if you can stand the pain.

Left

Timber battens are used to line the underside of the mezzanine. This lowered ceiling provides the kitchen and dining area with a scale and warmth appropriate for cooking and entertaining. The elegant folded steel stair is designed to intrude as little as possible into the open plan apartment while adding a sense of architectural drama to the space.

Case Study 2

Fleet Street Residence Sydney, New South Wales, Australia

Welsh + Major Architects was established by partners David Welsh and Chris Major as a full time practice in January 2004. For this transformation of a listed terrace house in a conservation area in Sydney, Australia, a dated ground floor living area built in the 1980s is replaced with a new volume that slides in to create a new kitchen, living and dining space, as well as a new courtyard and reading nook.

The roof of the insertion is manipulated to capture high-level light from three sides while a sequence of open and intimate internal and external spaces link the existing house with the new spaces. This volume will 'bookend' the rejuvenated rear garden with a new studio building, which replaces the garden shed and sets the garden and deck at the centre of the house.

The Fleet Street residence won the RAIA NSW Chapter Architecture Award 2007 for Small Projects.

David Welsh and Chris Major
Project Architects
Welsh + Major Architects

The commission for Fleet Street came about after the clients slipped a note under the door of another house we completed in a nearby suburb, whilst on a weekend bike ride. Their brief was to reconfigure the ground floor living spaces of a two storey terraced house built around 1900, including the reconfiguration of the ground floor living spaces, including kitchen, living, dining and bathroom areas, and the garden, as well as replacing a large garden shed with a studio.

The key components of the client brief were: to maximize the amount of natural light; to integrate the kitchen, dining and informal living spaces, including external areas; to enable cooking with a wok in the new integrated space without smoke and cooking smells invading the living spaces.

In addition, the clients had had first hand experience of traditional Beijing courtyard houses *(hutongs)* and so part of the brief was to integrate and adapt the existing and new spaces around the garden, using all of the available site area to create a series of internal and external rooms. The kitchen, as in a *hutong*, was to be a key component of this arrangement, with the flexibility to operate as an internal space, whilst also integrating it as part of the outdoor areas, depending on the season.

A series of joinery options were explored using banks of joinery in different configurations. The implemented scheme concentrated the main working components of the kitchen along the northern wall of the new space below a clerestory light set into a triangulated ceiling recess. Secondary elements of the kitchen such as a pull-out pantry, cookbook storage and a window seat were incorporated into another joinery volume which links the new

spaces with the formal lounge of the existing terrace. Bulk storage, broom cupboard and display space were integrated into the back of the adjacent bathroom box.

Hard wearing materials with visual warmth were part of the design brief. Tasmanian Oak (messmate) timber veneer boards with integrated solid timber handles were selected for all cupboard fronts (messmate, a native of south-eastern Australia is a managed, sustainable timber species) and Travertine was selected for the work surface material. Red colourback glass provides both a hardwearing splashback surface to the working areas, as well as a relief from the predominantly timber linings.

The builder was selected on the basis of his previous working relationship with the architect on the house that first gained the client's attention. Whilst a formal tender process was followed in selecting a builder, the fact that the architect and builder had collaborated on the house that first gained the client's attention was a key deciding factor in that selection. The joiner was in turn proposed by the builder based on their previous working relationship, and was asked to provide a price to complete the work. Their tender was then accepted by both client and architect. An important aspect of the design, both to us and to our client, was the inclusion of environmentally friendly materials and passive energy strategies. These included a water tank; recycled ironbark external decking and columns; internal flooring and timber veneers sourced from sustainable plantations; passive solar design principles utilized when organizing new spaces; and encouraging opportunities for cross ventilation.

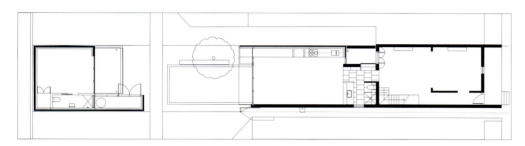

Above
Ground floor plan

Left
The principal working elements of the kitchen (left) are placed underneath a skylight that brings natural light into the kitchen and dining space. Tasmanian Oak is used for all of the joinery including two storage and display elements (centre and right). A vertical slot of clear glazed louvres opposite pivoting doors to the garden encourages cooling cross ventilation.

Stephen Corbett and Yeqin Zuo
Clients

A variety of kitchen options were presented by the architects. Ultimately, because of the restrictions in width – the house is only 4.5 metres (15 feet) wide internally, including the depth of the kitchen bench – a galley type of arrangement was decided upon. An integrated fridge only 650 millimetres (2 feet) deep was selected and purchased prior to construction beginning, which was fully integrated into the kitchen. The main concern of the brief for the kitchen was to be able to use a wok without smoking up the living and dining spaces. Also, we didn't want the kitchen to appear cold, particularly as it was likely to be part of the new living and dining areas. We also wanted the kitchen to be closely connected to the outside living spaces so that the kitchen, living, dining and garden areas would work well as one integrated space. These have now been organized and detailed to make the most of the temperate climate, the most important aspect of which is the garden, with all of the other spaces revolving around it.

Jason Boyle
Builder

The demarcation between builder and joiner (Provincial Kitchens) was blurred in this project due to the way that the kitchen relates to, and is integrated with, the architectural envelope. The integration of the kitchen into the new space demanded that the detailed cabinet work was undertaken by both us, as the builders, and the joiner working closely but on separate aspects of the design as a team.

The joiner concentrated on the carcasses, the cupboard fronts and the benchtops, including working with Tasmanian Oak to create solid handle profiles incorporated along one length of each operable panel, whether it be a drawer, cupboard, dishwasher or pull-out pantry. As the builders, we were responsible for the fixed panels, integration with the structure, wall and ceiling linings, the glass splashbacks and co-ordination of the appliances.

In addition, we were also responsible for the extension of the benchtop outside of the main kitchen that was designed to house a wok burner, and was constructed out of laminated marine-grade plywood. This bench required a connection that would be visible back to the main structure of the house, for stability. Rather than using a typical angle bracket solution, timber dowel was used to construct support pegs for the bench to rest on.

One of the key concerns and challenges of the project was the preparation of the travertine worktop. The selected stone was a particularly variegated type. Great attention was paid to the preparation, filling and polishing of the stone to a standard that was acceptable as a kitchen work surface. In the end the stone was filled and polished seven times over to achieve a finish that was suitable for a kitchen of this type.

Left
View of the kitchen and
dining space. Oak flooring
and cabinetry are relieved
by white-painted walls,
black steel beams and
column and the vibrant red
glass splashback. A custom-
made bench in the same
plane as the kitchen has
been created beyond the
folding glass doors to the
garden to create an area
for cooking with a wok –
a facility that the clients
particularly asked for.

Case Study 3

Private Apartment
London, England, UK

Claridge Architects was founded in June 2004. The practice has worked on residential, commercial and arts-related projects. The underlying philosophy of the practice can be described as 'Modern Minimalist' – keeping projects architecturally simple and ordered, creating elegant and functional design from the ambitions and briefs of their clients.

The design for this project consisted of the complete renovation of a seventh floor apartment in central London overlooking the Embankment, London Eye and the Houses of Parliament. The brief included the spatial reconfiguration and conversion of two neighbouring flats into one minimalist apartment, with the redesign encompassing four bathrooms, four bedrooms, utility room, living–dining room and kitchen.

Marcus Claridge
Architect
Claridge Architects
As modern kitchens are very personal spaces and often the most inhabited room in the house, I believe it is vital to fully involve the client in both the design process and choice of materials. As the client had a clear idea of what she wanted to achieve, the project ran very smoothly with few amendments. A few obstacles in the kitchen area influenced the design – these included two large units housing the air-conditioning equipment and commercial boiler that would have incurred massive costs if they had been relocated. As a result of having to incorporate these, a fully bespoke kitchen was the most viable option.

The kitchen was designed to be the centrepiece of the apartment and hence luxurious materials such as marble and walnut were selected, offset against the industrial feel of stainless steel. The initial kitchen discussions centred on a large rectangular island unit creating a visual barrier between the living area and the kitchen space, however there were reservations about pans and other cooking utensils being viewed from the living area.

This was eventually solved with the addition of a marble upstand around three sides of the island. The other deciding factor in the positioning of the kitchen was gaining the best possible view over the River Thames.

Materials were key to the success of the design. The Statuary marble we used creates a focal point, with the visual appeal of much larger veining than standard Carrara marble. As marble can have such random veining, the clients visited the stone yard themselves to choose the slab they wanted to use. Due to the problems with marble being porous, and therefore not suitable for the worktop, we chose a Snow White Zodiaq from Dupont. Unlike Corian this composite material has the feel and look of stone, but with the flexibility of Corian. Elsewhere in the kitchen, the deep grey of the marble was the deciding factor for the light, warm grey gloss lacquer finish of the joinery units, and the final touch was the introduction of a black ceramic hob and stainless steel appliances and square extractor. The simplicity of the extractor perfectly complements the geometric shapes of the kitchen.

The fully bespoke kitchen was manufactured by the main contractors off site, which meant we had full flexibility of design and no problem making amendments on site.

Stephen and Kathryn van Rooyen
Clients
We first met Claridge Architects in February of 2007 after a friend recommended them. The practice had a great mix of clients, and they had delivered retail and business projects as well as residential schemes. We were looking for someone that understood the simple contemporary style we liked but also someone who has an eye for the practicalities of everyday life. It was important to us to ensure that good storage was incorporated into the apartment and that the design would be thought through thoroughly to ensure things worked well. We wanted the apartment to look good but not at the cost of user friendliness.

The kitchen is really important to us and we had some pretty specific ideas in some areas and took advice in others. We knew the appliances must include an American-style double door fridge, a built-in coffee machine and a wine storage fridge and we knew we didn't want natural stone surfaces, as they would stain easily.

We wanted to make the most of the open plan as we have fantastic views. As the kitchen, dining and living areas are all open to each other,

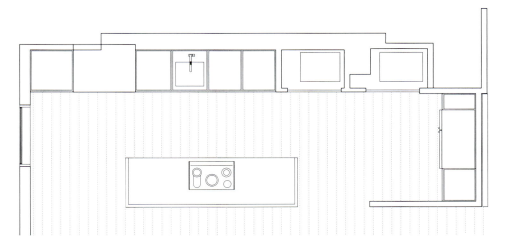

Above
Kitchen floor plan. The island unit forms the main focus of the kitchen, with large appliances such as the fridge-freezer and oven located in a recess to the right, and additional work space behind. The dimensions and location of this additional work space has been carefully designed to incorporate and hide the air-conditioning plant and boiler (right).

Left
The Statuary marble used for the upstand to the island unit and behind the worktop adds a truly luxurious and sophisticated touch to the otherwise simple and understated material palette and colour scheme.

it was important that the kitchen look smart and blend with the overall colour scheme. We chose a very pale grey for the cupboards and, while we were talking through how we could really make a statement with the area, my husband and the architect came up with the fabulous idea of making the lip around the island bench in marble with a matching feature wall above the sink behind the island. We both immediately thought of the same marble – Statuary – which is white with thick grey veins running through it. The effect, now that it is all installed, is even better than we had hoped. It looks fantastic and really makes the kitchen feel smarter and in keeping with the rest of the space.

Chris Milczanowski
Contractor
Floor 2 Ceiling

There were several challenges with constructing this kitchen, mainly access to the property. As it is a residential building, there were strict rules regarding the use of the lift and working times, which had to be adhered to. As with all bespoke kitchens, preparation is key, and everything has to be measured correctly. With this particular kitchen it was built off site, sprayed, constructed to make sure everything joined correctly and then disassembled for transit. This way we knew if any of the units didn't align, or were damaged before they got to site. Of course this doesn't guarantee that all the surfaces on site are going to align perfectly. Most of the units were a standard size, however some were slightly larger to fit into certain spaces. It was also important to get all final dimensions of the appliances beforehand, as these often govern unit sizes.

The apartment had to have a very clean, minimalist feel, with a very high-end finish throughout, and the kitchen was no exception. The handle-less doors and high gloss finish give clean lines to the kitchen, keeping it simple and unobtrusive and also not taking attention away from the primary materials and geometric shapes.

The large piece of marble on the rear wall was possibly the most difficult aspect of the kitchen to install. It was incredibly fragile and the edges can crumble easily. The weight was also a major consideration, especially when one has to carry it up seven flights of stairs. As this was such a large piece it had to be cut into two pieces and bonded together on site making sure the veining lined up perfectly.

The kitchen was successful because of its minimal finish, clean lines and use of extravagant materials. It is a beautifully designed kitchen which complements the rest of the apartment and creates an easy to use, social kitchen which has a wonderful view over London.

Stone Kitchens

Vincent Van Duysen Architects

M–VS Residence Brussels, Belgium

This larger than average apartment was created for a retired Dutch barrister and his wife who re-located to Brussels to create their new home. Fast connections to London, Amsterdam, Paris and Antwerp, where they had lived previously and have children, plus the cultural mix of Flemish and French that permeates the city, made it the obvious choice.

A key part of the brief for their new home was the accommodation of a collection of modern furniture including pieces by Eames, Bertoia and Eileen Gray. The client purchased two apartments in a newly built complex and asked Vincent Van Duysen to design the interior from the empty shells, including connecting the two spaces.

The finished apartment features a chequerboard of Carrara marble and dark oak which forms the palette throughout the space. Sliding walls, some in glass, some in oak, carve up the penthouse in a variety of configurations, with guest quarters and his and hers offices on the lower floor, connected by a marble spiral staircase. Splashes of colour, partly inspired by the furniture collection, feature in every room. In contrast, the kitchen is a haven of minimalism located in a slender space with sliding doors connecting it to the dining room. The main feature is a Carrara marble island bench which is matched by a custom designed overhead extractor and lighting

box, also clad in marble. The island accommodates ovens, hobs and sink, with larger appliances such as fridge and freezer, and large amounts of general pantry storage located in a wall of full-height cupboards ranged along the rear wall.

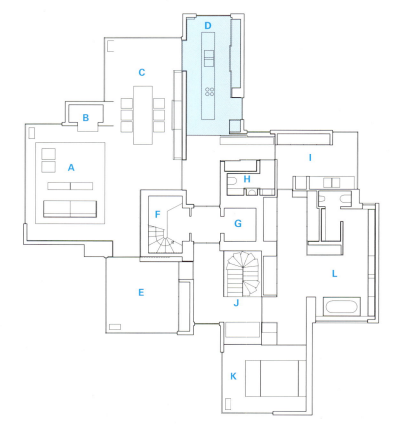

Opposite Left
View of the kitchen from the hallway. Large sliding panels open up the space to the adjacent dining room and Alvar Aalto stools allow guests to keep the chef company while preparation is underway.

Floor Plan
A Living room
B Fireplace
C Dining room
D Kitchen
E Library
F Fire stair
G Lift
H WC
 I Laundry
J Stair to lower floor
K Bedroom
L Dressing and master bathroom

Left
Every element of the kitchen is custom designed to create a beautifully calm and inviting space. Carrara marble is used for the flooring as well as for the island and overhead unit. The under-counter storage and cupboard doors have been sprayed to match the colour of the stone.

Stone

Vincent Van Duysen
M-VS Residence
Brussels, Belgium

**Kitchen Plan and Sections
A–A, B–B, and C–C
1:50**

1 Storage cupboards in
 dark oak veneer
2 Office / study storage in
 Carrara Statuario marble
3 Storage cupboard for
 microwave and steamer
4 Drawers in dark oak
 veneer

5 Refrigerator
6 Dishwasher
7 Custom-made stainless
 steel sink
8 Gas hob
9 Carrara Statuary marble
 worktop
10 Carrara Statuary marble
 floor tiles
11 Full-height glazed
 window

12 Custom sized Carrara
 Statuario marble wall
 cladding
13 Extractor unit with matte
 glazed cover
14 Gas oven
15 Disposal unit
16 Lacquered MDF sliding
 door to rear wall
17 Under-sink storage
 cupboard

18 Lacquered MDF sliding
 door

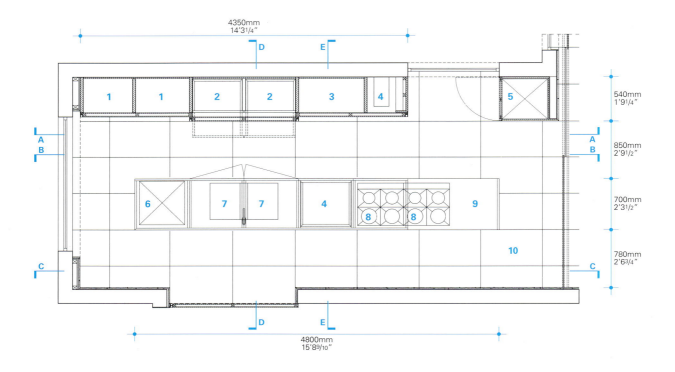

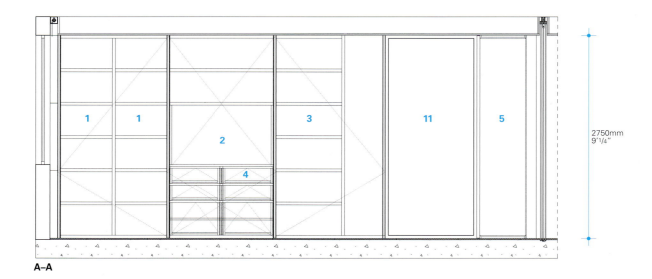

A–A

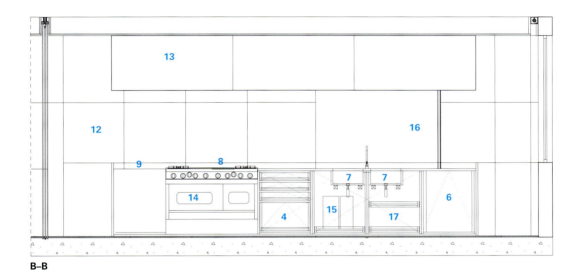

B–B

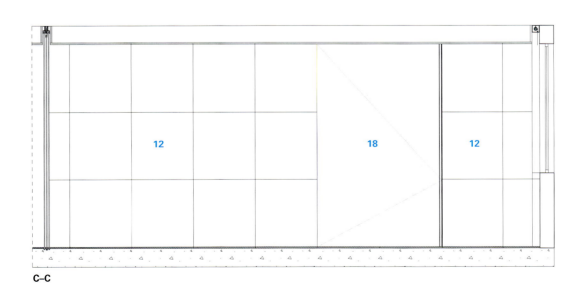

C–C

Stone

Vincent Van Duysen
M-VS Residence
Brussels, Belgium

**Kitchen Sections
D–D and E–E
1:20**

1 Custom sized Carrara
   Statuario marble wall
   cladding
2 Extractor unit with matte
   glazed cover
3 Glazed window
4 Chrome mixer tap
5 Custom made Carrara
   Statuario marble front
   panel to island unit
6 Custom made stainless
   steel sink
7 Disposal unit
8 Lacquered MDF sliding
   door
9 Storage cupboards in
   dark oak veneer
10 Office / study storage in
   Carrara Statuario marble
11 Drawers in dark oak
   veneer
12 Carrara Statuario marble
   floor tiles
13 Custom made Carrara
   Statuario marble worktop

D–D

Materials
Worktop Carrara Statuario marble custom made worktop
Joinery MDF with dark oak veneer
Floor 50 x 80 mm (2 x 3 inch) Carrara Statuary marble floor tiles
Lighting Tekna custom made TL fittings

Appliances and Fixtures
Taps Vola KV1 mixer tap and spout
Sink Custom made Inox stainless steel sink
Disposal Unit Franke sorter 600/450
Dishwasher Miele G658 SCVi
Refrigerator Miele KF 304i
Hob Viking EVGIC485-4GQ
Oven Viking EVGIC485-4GQ
Microwave Miele
Steam Oven Miele
Extractor Venduro custom made extractor

Project Credits
Completion 2001
Project Architects Vincent Van Duysen, Stephanie Laperre, Sophie Laenen
Main Contractor Potteau Interiors
General Contractor De Coene Decor / Bouwkantoor Dedeyne
Structural Engineers Bouquet-Deloof
Lighting Consultant TEKNA bvba

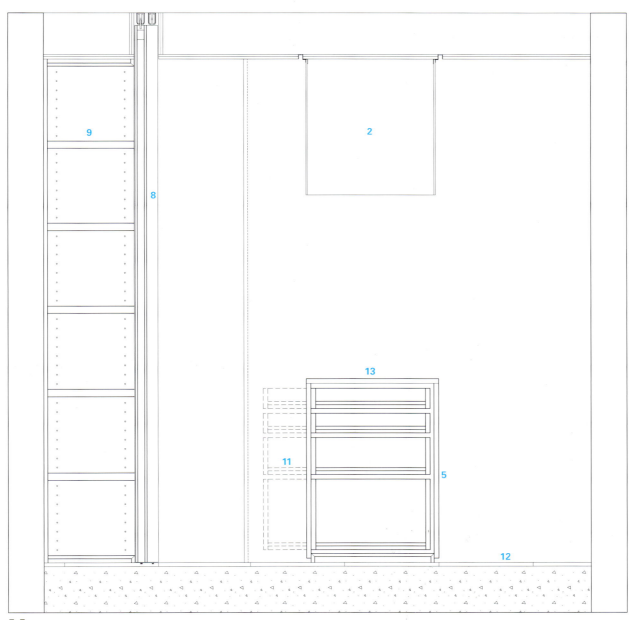

E–E

Architectenlab BVBA

House M
Limburg, Belgium

House M is conceived as a family home in which the design focuses on privacy without sacrificing natural light or space. At the front of the house, the façade draws back from the street in two steps to create a carport and a private entrance. The same principle is applied at the centre of the house where a private courtyard is located.

With walls of full-height sliding glass panels, an abundance of natural light is allowed into the rooms surrounding this open space which doubles the living area in summer when both sets of doors are open.

The beautifully simple kitchen looks directly onto the dining area, and is defined by a lowered ceiling that forms the floor of a mezzanine reading area on the first floor. Because of the limited floor area and building restrictions, spaces had to be kept compact, which is also true for the kitchen. However, the clean lines and simplicity of the components – principally a low floating island bench and a length of full-height storage cupboards – give no clue to the way that every square inch of available space has been maximized to full effect.

The open plan part of the kitchen is connected to a storage and laundry area which has its own entrance so that groceries do not have to be carried through the main part of the house. Storage and cooking facilities are situated in full-height cupboards behind an island unit and are painted the same colour as the walls so that only when open do they reveal the generous storage as well as the refrigerator, gas hob and extractor unit. As a result, even when in use, the kitchen does not appear to be a typical cooking area, but serves more as an extended part of the dining area. The island houses a dishwasher, washing and preparation area and is designed to appear as a monolithic piece of furniture sculpted from Belgian Bleu stone.

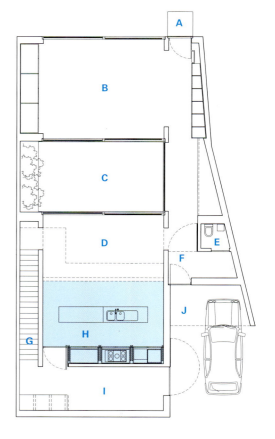

Opposite Left
View of the main entrance where a bridge at first floor level provides cover to the carport. From here, the kitchen is accessed either via the entrance hall or through the utility area on the left.

Floor Plan
A Entrance
B Living room
C Courtyard
D Dining room
E WC
F Entrance
G Stair
H Kitchen
I Utility
J Carport

Left
A monolithic stone-clad island bench provides the focus for the kitchen. The clean lines are interrupted only by a recessed stainless steel double sink unit, and are emphasized by the neutrality of the full-height storage cupboards behind. A bank of adjustable halogen lights and hanging fluorescents provide high quality task lighting.

Above
The kitchen overlooks the dining area, and the courtyard beyond which is the focus of the living spaces. The living room beyond is still connected to the kitchen via the sliding glass doors that delineate the courtyard.

Stone

Architectenlab BVBA
House M
Limburg, Belgium

**Kitchen Island
Plan, Kitchen Island
Carcass Plan, Elevation A
and Sections A–A and B–B
1:50**
1 Belgian Bleu stone
  worktop
2 Stainless steel double
  sink
3 Belgian Bleu stone
  integral sink drainer

4 Spray-painted MDF
  cupboard carcass
5 Under-sink area
6 Dishwasher
7 Belgian Bleu stone island
  cladding
8 Spray-painted MDF
  drawer fronts
9 Spray-painted MDF
  cupboard fronts
10 Stainless steel mixer tap

11 Electrical socket to front
  of bench
12 Kitchen towel storage

**Kitchen Cupboards
Plan, Elevation A,
Sections A–A, B–B and C–C
1:50**
1 Refrigerator
2 Combination microwave
  oven

3 Gas hob
4 Folding and sliding
  pocket doors
5 Crockery cupboard
6 Pivot door to utility room
7 Spray-painted MDF
  cupboard fronts
8 Spray-painted MDF
  pocket doors
9 Integrated door handles
10 Extractor unit behind

cupboard front
11 Spray-painted MDF
  carcass
12 MDF shelves to crockery
  cupboard
13 Stainless steel cupboard
  door

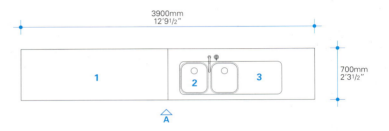

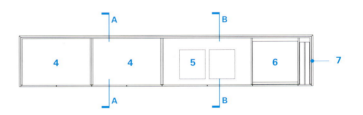

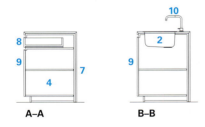

A–A   B–B

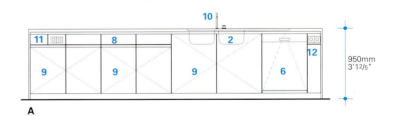

A

32

Materials
Worktop Belgian bleu stone
Joinery Spray-painted MDF
Floor Polished concrete
Lighting KREON double mini downlights (qr-cb kr972553) to kitchen cupboards. LIGHT u-line 'Maarten van Severen' HA-228 to kitchen island. Lucitalia kriter 10-06090 to dining area

Appliances and Fixtures
Tap and Spout VOLA 590 in stainless steel
Sink Franke Exquiso AMX 110.340
Dishwasher Siemens SE 35592 integrated dishwasher
Refrigerator Siemens integrated refrigerator with stainless steel finish
Hob Siemens ER 19050 EU
Combination Microwave Oven Siemens HB 77 L 55EU
Extractor Novy D 888 integrated extractor unit

Project Credits
Completion 2003
Client Mr and Mrs Tom Martens and An-Katrien Piot
Project Architects Peter-Paul Piot, William Froidmont, Bart America
Structural Engineers MEBO bvba
Services Engineer Architectenlab
Quantity Surveyor Architectenlab
Lighting Consultant Crea Luce

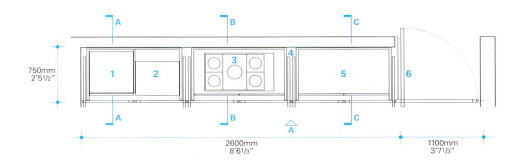

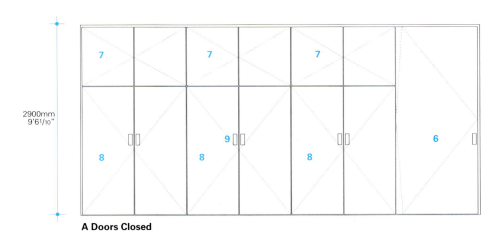

A Doors Closed

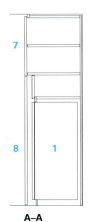

A–A

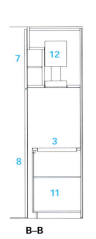

B–B

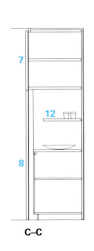

C–C

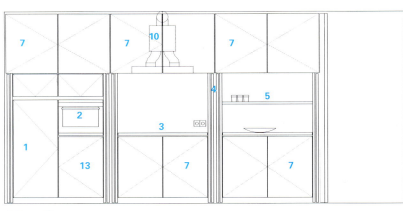

A Doors Open

Turner Castle

Slat House
London, England, UK

This project involves the extension and remodelling of a 1930s end of terrace house in South London, referred to for its unusual use of timber cladding, as the Slat House. The client specified an extension which would open up the interior of the house during the summer, making a greater connection to the garden.

They also wanted a 'tough' and flexible series of internal spaces, which are able to adapt to the changing needs of a growing family. On the ground floor an expansive space is cut through the house, creating a vista from the entrance through to the rear garden. The spaces can be separated and reconfigured with large sliding panels.

The new extension houses a large kitchen and dining area with in situ concrete floors and walls and a bespoke concrete worktop and breakfast bar. A dramatic new window frames the garden and a large sliding door gives access to the new terrace. A new room at the front of the extension, lined with birch-faced plywood, functions as a work studio and garage, accessed from the front via a giant swing door.

The internal finishes of the extension are pulled through into the main house, emphasizing the new open plan arrangement of the ground floor. Timber cladding was specified as a practical necessity to reduce the load of the building on its new foundations,

but also for aesthetic purposes, to harmonize the extension with its wooded surroundings. The width of the red cedar panels defined a module by which all window and door openings were determined. This rigour adds to the strong exterior appearance of the building.

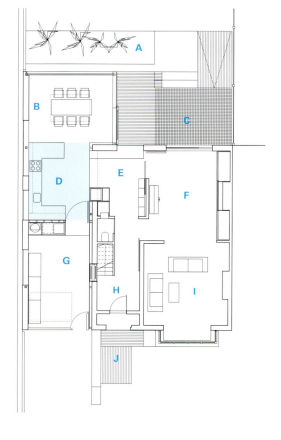

Opposite Left
The timber-clad extension is attached to the side of the existing house where it adds much needed open plan space to this family home. Here, the open door leads into a garage and studio and beyond to the kitchen, which in turn leads to the dining area and the garden.

Floor Plan
A Garden
B Dining room
C Terrace
D Kitchen
E Library
F Music and play room
G Garage and studio
H Entrance hall
I Living room
J Entrance

Left
The simple and robust kitchen features cantilevered timber-fronted cupboards and a custom made polished concrete worktop notched into the wall.

Bottom Left
View from the kitchen towards the dining area which is flooded with natural light from a wall of frameless glazing overlooking the garden and a skylight above.

Stone

Turner Castle
Slat House
London, England, UK

Kitchen Plan, Elevation A and Section B–B
1:50

1 Door from garage and studio
2 80 mm (3 inch) thick polished concrete worktop
3 Concealed fluorescent tube lighting in high level window with exterior timber slats
4 Undermounted stainless steel sink
5 Dishwasher
6 Stainless steel gas hob
7 Polished concrete worktop on concrete leg
8 Dining room
9 Glazed wall to garden
10 Opening to library
11 Cantilevered concrete shelf with undermounted lighting
12 Aluminium tap
13 Cantilevered base units with burnt oak multi-ply doors on push catches
14 Drawers with burnt oak multi-ply fronts
15 Extractor concealed in plywood box
16 Stainless steel flush-faced electrical socket cast in wall
17 Cast concrete leg
18 Polished concrete wall cast in panels against phenolic plywood

Right
View of the kitchen from the library. Polished concrete floors and worktop are contrasted with the warmth of the timber cladding and door frames.

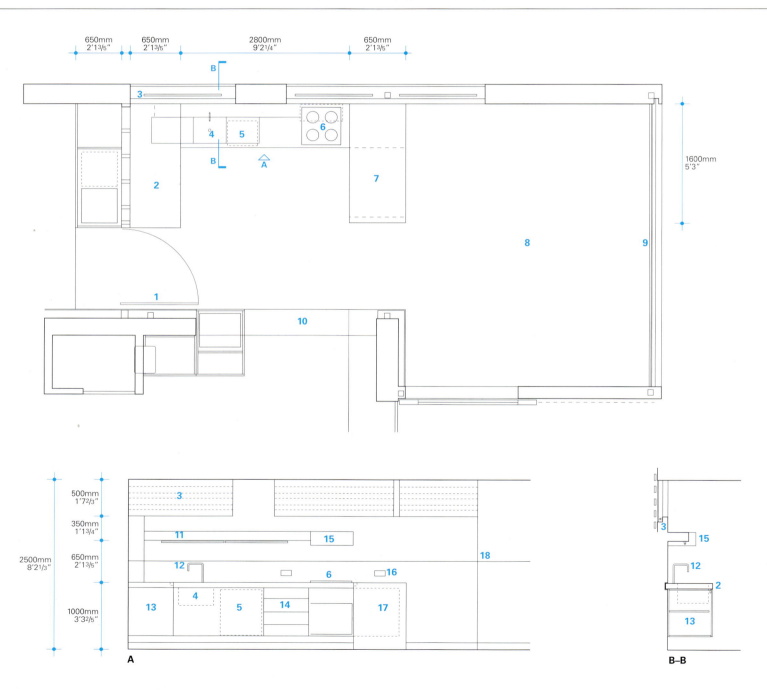

Materials
Worktop 80 mm (3¹/10 inch) thick polished concrete
Joinery Phenolic plywood kitchen base units with burnt oak multi-ply doors
Floor 75 mm (3 inch) thick concrete screed with embedded heating pipes
Walls Smooth concrete linings cast against phenolic ply formwork in horizontal panels

Appliances and Fixtures
Taps Brushed aluminium mixer tap and spout from Habitat
Sink Under-mounted stainless steel sink by Smeg
Dishwasher Mini-dishwasher by Miele
Refrigerator Tall, integrated Miele refrigerator
Hob Smeg four burner stainless steel gas hob
Oven Smeg stainless steel single oven
Extractor Smeg 600 mm (23²/3 inch) wide extractor
Lighting Surface mounted and concealed 110 watt architectural tubes by Compton and recessed adjustable low voltage spot lights

Project Credits
Completion 2006
Project Architects Carl Turner, Cassion Castle, Alicja Borkowska, Kirsty Yaldron
Structural Engineers Wright Consultancy Group
Main Contractor Turner Castle

Crepain Binst Architecture (Luc Binst)

Lofthouse Humbeek, Belgium

This private house is a sculptural synthesis of the client's personal creativity and an interpretation of the flexibility of a loft space. The design avoids a room-based approach, in which the enjoyment of the house invariably results in a fragmented setting. Instead, everything is organized as one large space, in which everything interrelates.

The house is constructed entirely from concrete, supported on fins of solid sheet steel, with a substantial cantilevered element. The two split-level floors allow the integration of the programme into the volume and create the required visual relationships. From the living space one is in contact with the carport, and from the carport with the office, the entrance

hall and the living space. The composition of these relationships enables a considerable degree of visual control over the organization of the house.

For example, the office worktop, 13.5 metres (44 feet) in length, becomes a concrete catwalk anchored in the wall like a suspended plinth. The monumental black access stairs to the living space provide an advance announcement of the shift in scale, which is especially evident in the living space. The kitchen island becomes a multifunctional object in the space. On the same axis lies the larger than average shower, looking out over the entire living space, which is given a central place in the dwelling.

The kitchen consists of a single large marble island unit with an integrated light panel, and a white, gloss-finished cantilevered wall unit in which all of the appliances are fitted, including the hob. Horizontal ribbon windows are located above and below the wall unit, adding to the illusion that the joinery is floating.

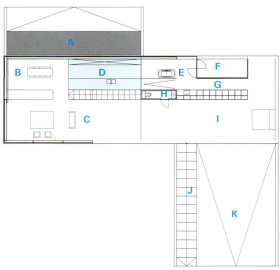

Opposite Left

The 200 millimetre (7 3/4 inch) thick structural concrete skin of the façade is, unusually, coated in black cement which is attached to the frame using a ventilated cavity system. The two pictograms on the front of the house symbolize the humanity of architecture in the form of two filters over the sliding windows. These touches also represent an allusion to the abstraction of this project.

Floor Plan

A Terrace
B Dining area
C Living area
D Kitchen
E Bathroom
F Terrace
G Dressing area
H WC
I Bedroom
J Stair from garage below
K Ramp from garage below

Above Left

The large island bench features a virtually seamless marble countertop with integrated Corian double sink and recessed drainage areas.

Below Left

The front vertical surface of the island unit, facing the living area, incorporates an electrically operated RGB wall that changes colour according to pre-set patterns, or according to the mood of the inhabitants.

Stone

Crepain Binst Architecture (Luc Binst)
Lofthouse
Humbeek, Belgium

**Kitchen Plan
1:50**

1 MDF storage cupboard with white epoxy-spray finish
2 Integrated refrigerator
3 Integrated freezer
4 Hob
5 Built-in oven and microwave
6 MDF white epoxy-sprayed three drawer unit with marble fronts
7 MDF white epoxy-sprayed two drawer unit with marble fronts
8 Integrated dishwasher
9 White Corian double sink integrated into Carrara Venato marble worktop
10 MDF white epoxy-sprayed four drawer unit with marble fronts
11 Philips RGB light wall
12 Jet black Indian marble stairs

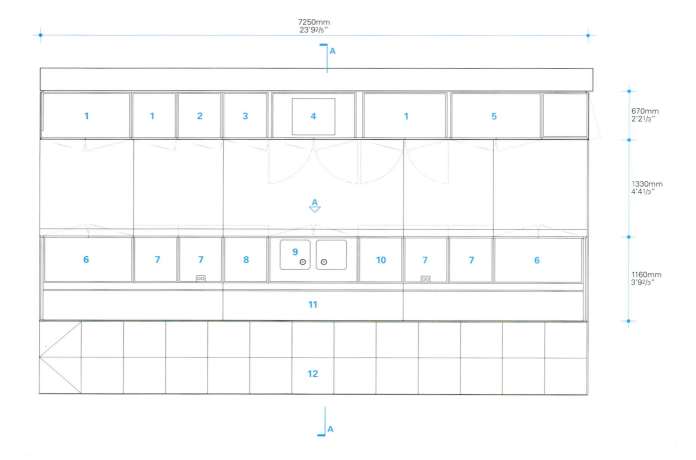

**Kitchen Island Elevation A
1:50**

1 Steel deck roof construction
2 Carrara Venato marble worktop
3 MDF white epoxy-sprayed three drawer unit with marble fronts
4 MDF white epoxy-sprayed two drawer unit with marble fronts
5 MDF white epoxy-sprayed four drawer unit with marble fronts
6 White Corian double sink integrated into Carrara Venato marble worktop
7 Stainless steel spout and mixer tap
8 Integrated dishwasher
9 Blue light line between epoxy floor and cabinet

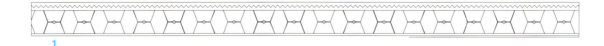

1

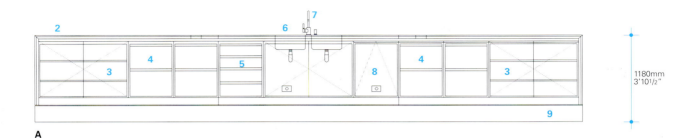

2   6   7

4
5
3   8   4   3

1180mm
3'10 1/2"

9

A

Stone

Crepain Binst Architecture (Luc Binst)
Lofthouse
Humbeek, Belgium

Section A–A
1:50

1 Black cement-coated concrete exterior skin
2 Aluminium-framed floor level window
3 Steel deck roof
4 White epoxy poured floor
5 Jet black Indian marble stair
6 Philips RGB light wall
7 Carrara Venato marble worktop
8 Stainless steel spout and mixer tap
9 MDF white epoxy-sprayed drawer unit with marble front
10 Blue light line between epoxy floor and cabinet
11 White epoxy-sprayed wall unit
12 Extractor fan
13 Aluminium-framed ceiling level window
14 Integrated hob

Right
The highly crafted marble island bench also features marble drawer and cupboard fronts. The highly polished work surface reflects elements of the living space (right) and the glass-enclosed bathroom and terrace beyond.

Far Right Above
Detail view of the taps and spout which are surface-mounted in the marble countertop.

Far Right Below
Detail view of the mitred corners and handle-free drawer fronts of the marble island bench.

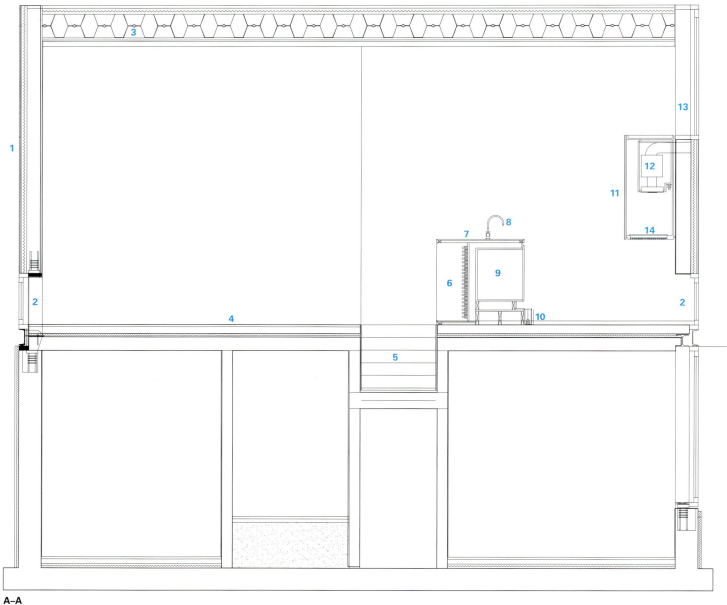

A–A

Materials
Worktop Polished Carrara Venato marble
Joinery White gloss-finished wall units supplied and installed by Beneens
Floor Blue epoxy poured floor manufactured by Bevers bvba

Appliances and Fixtures
Taps and Spout Dornbracht
Sink Custom-made white Corian double under-mounted sink
Dishwasher Smeg
Washing Machine Smeg
Refrigerator Smeg
Hob Smeg
Oven Smeg
Microwave Smeg
Extractor Novy
Lighting Philips RGB light wall and blue light line

Project Credits
Completion 2004
Client Luc Binst
Interior Designer Luc Binst, Tom de Meester
Structural Engineers Bas bvba
Main Contractor Janssens bvba
Quantity Surveyor Luc Binst

John Pawson

Tetsuka House
Tokyo, Japan

This minimalist house is located on a constricted site in a suburb to the south-west of Tokyo. Extremely high land values and demanding building regulations to cope with the risk of earthquakes have not dampened a design that expresses traditional and contemporary aspects of Japanese domestic life.

The elegant two-storey box turns its back on its surroundings, creating instead a tranquil inner calm. Constructed from rendered and painted concrete, the box is pierced by only a few glazed openings in order to edit out the outside world. Spaces for living, dining and cooking are located on the ground floor, while sleeping, bathing and dressing areas upstairs

are reached by a single flight of stairs. Throughout, a limited palette of materials – limestone, plaster, concrete, timber and glass – reinforces the formal rigour of the architecture.

A secluded courtyard with a single Japanese maple forms the focus for the entire house. The main living space faces directly onto the courtyard, as does a tea ceremony room with traditional tatami mat floor. The boundary between the internal spaces and the courtyard are blurred via panes of full-height glazing and a stone bench that seamlessly traverses the length of the house.

While the courtyard has the prosaic function of filtering out the nondescript suburban

context, more importantly it serves to frame elements of the landscape – a trace of sky, branches of the tree – in the manner of traditional Japanese landscape design. The kitchen is located at one end of the living space and is comprised of a wall of full-height storage cupboards and a simple stone island unit that houses the sink and hob. From the living room, the only accent in the otherwise perfect minimalism of the kitchen is an elegant stainless steel spout that rises above the edge of the kitchen island upstand.

Opposite Left
The plain exterior to the house is designed to protect the privacy of the inhabitants, and to give preference to an internal domestic life in which the main spaces look out to a walled courtyard rather than to the urban context.

Floor Plan
A Entrance
B Kitchen storage wall
C Kitchen island
D Dining table
E Entrance hall
F Stair to first floor
G Living room
H WC
I Shower
J Tea room
K Courtyard

Left
The kitchen is in keeping with the calm asceticism that characterizes the entire house. A single stainless steel spout rises from the stone worktop. An upstand to the worktop conceals cooking activity from the adjacent living space, and the worktop projects on a single blade support to create an integrated dining table.

Stone

John Pawson
Tetsuka House
Tokyo, Japan

Kitchen Island
Plan and Elevations A, B, C
1:20
1 Limestone countertop
  and dining table
2 White-painted MDF
  support panel under
  dining table
3 Hob
4 Stone-clad upstand to
  island between kitchen

and living room
5 Integrated dishwasher
6 Stainless steel spout
7 Stainless steel sink
8 Stainless steel tap
9 White-painted MDF
  door panel
10 Stone-clad splashback
11 Line of stainless steel
   sink behind
12 Shadow line between

countertop and support
panel
13 Line of limestone
   upstand wall beyond

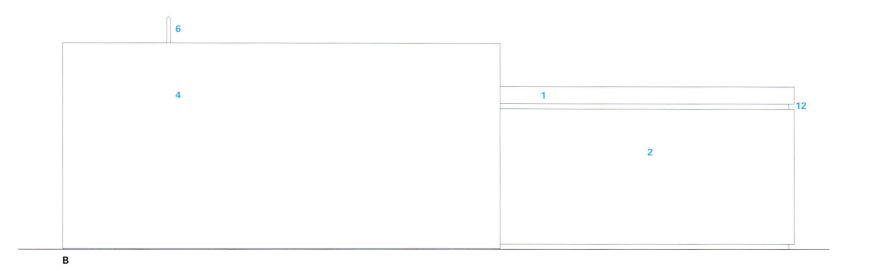

B

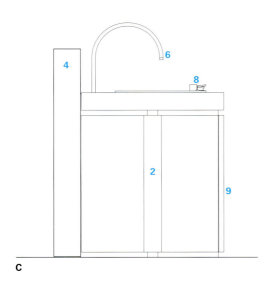

C

Stone

John Pawson
Tetsuka House
Tokyo, Japan

Kitchen Storage
Elevation and Plans
1:50
1 Washing machine
2 Toaster
3 Coffee maker
4 Rice steamer
5 Equipment drawers
6 Refrigerator
7 Adjustable MDF shelves
8 Freezer

9 Microwave oven
10 Steam oven
11 Knife and cutlery drawer
12 Washing machine with
   storage above
13 Appliance cupboard
14 Microwave, steam oven
   and storage
15 Equipment storage

Right
View of the kitchen from the
living area. A full-height run
of white cupboards conceal
both kitchen appliances
(refrigerator, microwave,
steam oven) as well as
laundry equipment and
pantry storage.

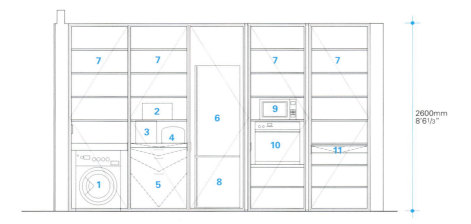

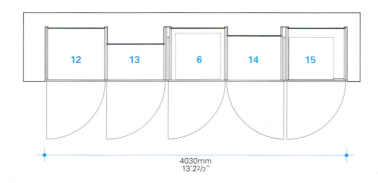

Materials
Worktop Limestone
Joinery White-painted MDF
Floor Polished concrete

Appliances and Fixtures
Taps Vola
Spout Bespoke chrome spout
Sink Bespoke undermounted stainless steel sink
Dishwasher Miele
Washing Machine Miele
Refrigerator Miele
Hob Gaggenau
Oven Miele
Microwave Miele
Extractor Gaggenau

Project Credits
Completion 2005
Client Katsuhiko and Yumiko Tetsuka
Project Team John Pawson, Vishwa Kaushal, Shingo Ozawa
General Contractor Nakajima Corporation

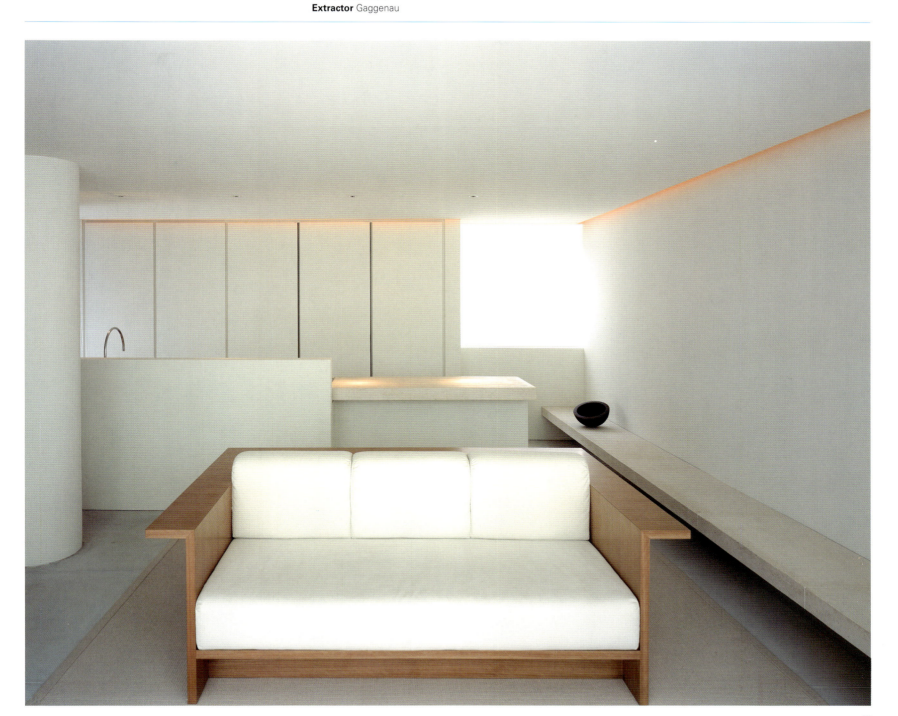

Lippmann Associates

Pearl Beach House
Pearl Beach, New South Wales, Australia

This 420 square metre (4,521 square foot) house is located on the stunning Pearl Beach waterfront at the foot of Mount Ettalong on the central coast of New South Wales. The house is orientated to face the ocean while simultaneously taking in the stunning escarpment of the adjacent mountain range.

The plan consists of a series of steel 'pods' arranged around a central courtyard, which provides relief from harsh winds and excessive sun. Sliding doors provide access into the courtyard from all sides.

On the upper level a private retreat is provided by a master bedroom, ensuite and study. The roofscape consists of a series of flat and sloping roofs (both flat gravel roofs and pitched corrugated steel) which permit maximum solar penetration while excluding the cold in winter.

The steel framing is clad with fibre cement wall panelling. Internally, timber floors and door fronts are combined with stone joinery to provide an environment which contributes to its context while maintaining the casual feel of a beach house.

The kitchen is located at one end of a spacious open plan dining and living space that looks out over the garden and views of the ocean. It is arranged as a run of stainless steel worktop and splashback against the end wall with storage cupboards above and below, extending into a full-height section to house an integrated fridge-freezer and pantry, and an island bench featuring a luxurious and richly variegated red marble worktop and side panels. A dining table sitting parallel to the island features the same Rosso Laguna stone.

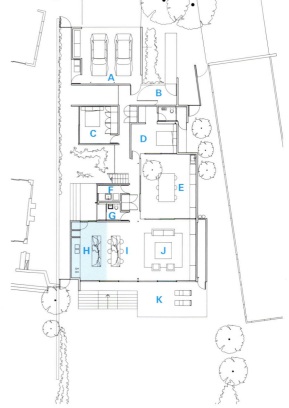

Opposite Left
The kitchen and dining area (left) are positioned to take full advantage of both direct access to the garden via a terrace, and views beyond to the ocean.

Floor Plan
A Garage
B Entrance
C Bedroom
D Bedroom
E Courtyard
F Laundry
G WC
H Kitchen
I Dining area
J Living area
K Terrace

Above
Full-height sliding glass doors open up the entire ground floor to the landscape. The kitchen itself is arranged as a wall of worktop with overhead cupboards against the wall, and an island bench facing the dining and living areas.

Stone

Lippmann Associates
Pearl Beach House
Pearl Beach, New South
Wales, Australia

**Kitchen Plan
1:50**
1 Fully integrated fridge-
 freezer
2 Pull-out pantry cupboards
3 Stainless steel double
 sink with cast-in drainage
 channels
4 Stainless steel
 countertop
5 Gas hob

6 Euromarble 'Rosso
 Laguna' stone
 countertop to island unit
7 Euromarble 'Rosso
 Laguna' stone dining
 table
8 Full-height sliding glass
 doors

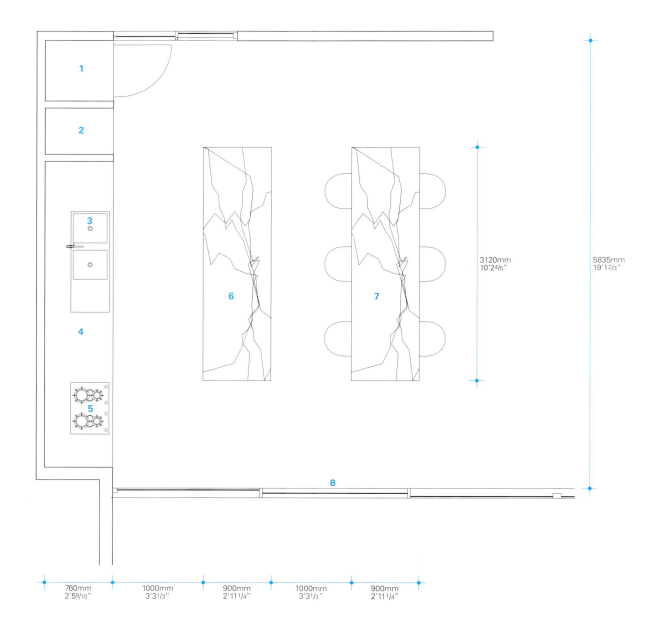

3120mm
10'2⁴/₅"

5835mm
19'1²/₃"

760mm
2'5⁹/₁₀"

1000mm
3'3¹/₃"

900mm
2'11¹/₄"

1000mm
3'3¹/₃"

900mm
2'11¹/₄"

Kitchen Counter Plan, Elevation A and Section A–A
1:50

1. Gas hob
2. Stainless steel double sink with cast-in drainage channels
3. Stainless steel countertop
4. Pull-out pantry cupboards
5. Fully integrated fridge-freezer
6. Polyurethane spray finish to cupboard front
7. Adjustable MDF shelf
8. Rangehood
9. Stainless steel power point to underside of cupboard
10. Full height sliding glass doors
11. Polyurethane spray finish to drawer fronts
12. Oven
13. Dishwasher
14. Recycling and waste bins under double stainless steel sink
15. Cabinet lights and power outlets under bulkhead
16. Stainless steel splashback integral with countertop
17. Return air grille at kickplate

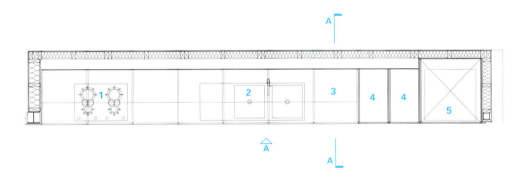

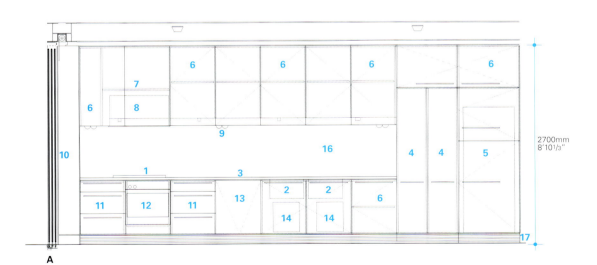

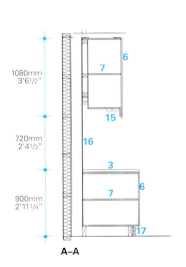

Stone

Lippmann Associates
Pearl Beach House
Pearl Beach, New South
Wales, Australia

**Island Countertop Plan,
Elevation A and Section
A–A
1:20**
1 Euromarble 'Rosso
   Laguna' stone
   countertop
2 Line of sprayed
   polyurethane cabinets
   under
3 Microwave under built

into joinery
4 Chopping board storage
   under
5 Euromarble 'Rosso
   Laguna' stone side panel
6 Polyurethane spray
   finish to drawer fronts
7 Return air ventilation
   grille
8 Euromarble 'Rosso
   Laguna' stone to under-

bench panel
9 Polyurethane spray
   finish to under-bench
   panel
10 MDF drawer

Right
View of the kitchen looking
out to magnificent views of
the ocean. White sprayed
cupboard and drawer fronts
are complemented by
simple stainless steel D-pull
handles.

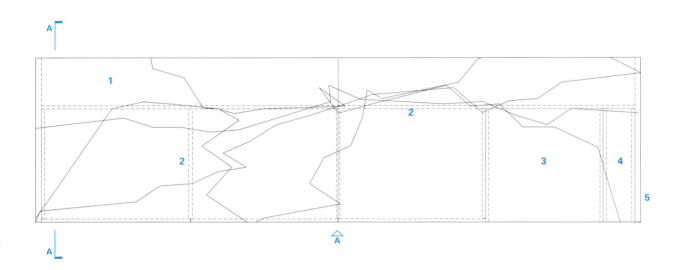

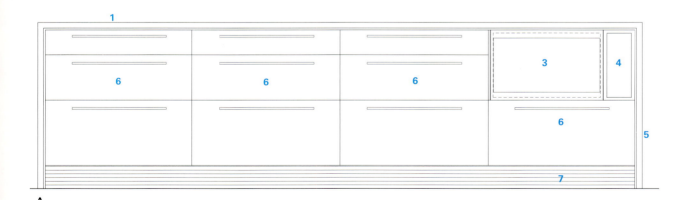

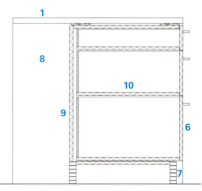

A

A–A

Materials
Worktop 30 mm (1 1/5 inch) thick Rosso Laguna marble
Joinery Polyurethane sprayed MDF and melamine
Floor Tongue and groove Blackbutt timber

Appliances and Fixtures
Taps and Spouts Vola KVI
Sink Integrated stainless steel sink
Refrigerator Fully integrated fridge-freezer
Hob Smeg
Oven Smeg
Microwave Qasar
Lighting Concealed 36 watt fluorescent strips

Project Credits
Completion 2004
Client Grant Johnstone
Project Architects Ed Lippmann, Jason Wedesweiler,
Kim Vandenberg
Structural Engineer Taylor Thomson Whitting
Services Engineer Lippmann Associates
Main Contractor Les Moore Projects
Lighting Consultant Lippmann Associates
Landscape Architect Lippmann Associates

Levitate Architecture and Design Studio

Nicklin House
London, England, UK

This luminous kitchen is part of an extensive plan to resolve common-place inadequacies typical to this type of Edwardian semi-detached house. While presenting an attractive double-fronted façade with reception rooms either side of a central hall, the rear of the property was poorly planned.

Both living room and kitchen sat deep within the plan, around a dark contorted corridor, hidden from the garden by a lean-to conservatory and dining room. The architect's response was simple: to clear away accretions and provide a single volume that could unify living, dining and kitchen space with the south-easterly garden.

A shallow-pitch rooflight runs across the entire width, bringing order to the elevation and flooding the new interior with light. Baffled by a bi-axial frosted perspex canopy, the space is constantly animated by a shifting pattern of light and shade. Creating a level soffit, the canopy is mirrored externally to provide shade and privacy. A lateral service core contains storage and a WC, while two symmetrical piers provide structural and spatial resolution, defining space for living, dining and cooking.

At the east end of the new space the kitchen comprises two principal elements – a single run of units set along the flanking wall with hob and sink, and a dramatic cantilevered island unit anchored to one of the piers. Grounded by an integrated oven set against the pier, a three metre (10 feet) long work surface cantilevers at either end. Seen from dining and living areas, the unit appears to hover above the floor.

To achieve this, a 300 millimetre (1 foot) deep steel truss cantilevers out and is cloaked by sprayed panels that match the wall units. The whole installation is topped with a Zodiaq composite stone countertop in Chalk White. Concealed lighting serves to reinforce the illusion of levitation.

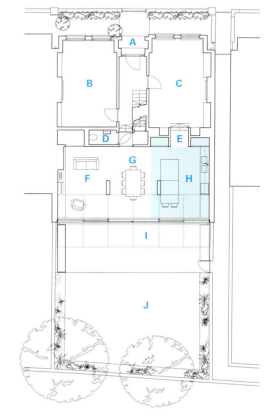

Opposite Left
View of the transforming extension from the garden. The living area, dining room and kitchen (from left to right respectively) are placed under a bi-axial louvred canopy of perspex which extends out over the garden terrace.

Floor Plan
A Entrance
B Reception room 1
C Reception room 2
D WC
E Stair down to kitchen
F Living room
G Dining room
H Kitchen
I Canopy over terrace
J Garden

Left
Placed against the side wall of the house, the kitchen consists of a run of worktop including the sink and hob, with overhead cupboards extending up to the ceiling. In front, a partly cantilevered island unit with matching stone worktop and sprayed cupboard fronts is anchored to the floor slab.

Bottom Left
View from the living room. The south-east facing wall of sliding glass doors brings abundant natural light into the living, dining and kitchen areas, while the baffled canopy casts a tracery of shadow across the space.

Kitchen Plan and Sections A–A and B–B
1:50
1 Pantry cupboard
2 Sink drainer
3 Stainless steel sink
4 Gas hob
5 Composite stone worktop with cupboards under
6 Stair from reception

room
7 Storage cupboards to dining room
8 Cantilevered composite stone worktop to island unit
9 Line of integrated oven below
10 Structural pillar
11 Full-height glazing
12 Polyurethane sprayed

cupboard fronts with adjustable shelving behind
13 Integrated extractor unit
14 Perspex baffles to skylight
15 Chrome mixer tap and spout
16 Integrated dishwasher
17 Concealed lighting
18 Polyurethane sprayed

drawer fronts
19 End panel to island unit
20 Composite stone worktop to island unit
21 Glass splashback

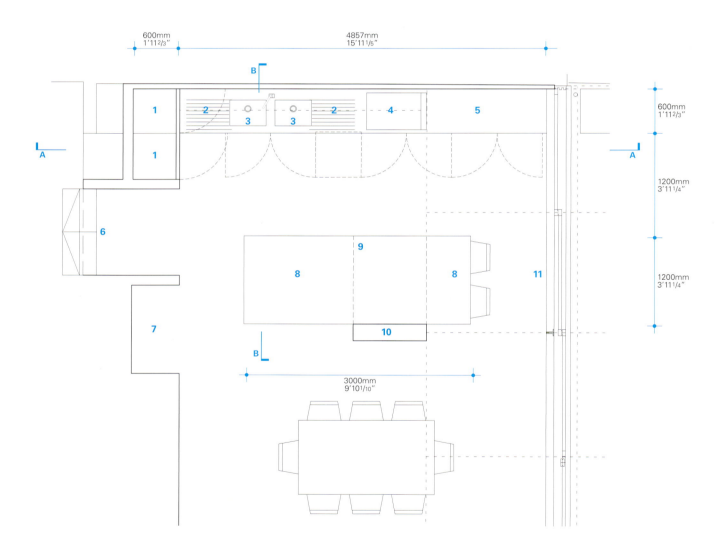

2635mm
8'7³/4"

1100mm
3'7¹/3"

600mm
1'11²/3"

935mm
3'4/5"

12   12

1

13

15   21

2   4

3   3   16

12   12   12

14

A–A

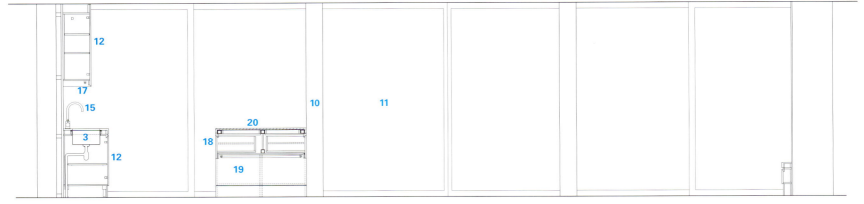

12

17

15

3

12

20

18

19

10   11

B–B

Stone

Levitate Architecture and Design Studio
Nicklin House
London, England, UK

Island Unit
Plan and Section
1:20

1 Polyurethane sprayed drawer in open position
2 Drawer under
3 Built-in oven under
4 Composite stone worktop on ply substrate
5 20 x 20 mm (3/4 x 3/4 inch) steel bar leg

6 Line of 50 x 50 mm (2 x 2 inch) square hollow section
7 Steel truss behind drawers, under worktop
8 Cupboard below
9 Structural pillar
10 Sprayed MDF end panel
11 Cantilevered drawer unit
12 Concealed fluorescent light fitting

13 Truss formed from 16 mm diameter steel rod between 50 x 50 mm (2 x 2 inch) square hollow section
14 50 x 50 mm (2 x 2 inch) square hollow section frame to worktop
15 Timber blocking to sprayed MDF kickplate
16 Bracket bolting steel

frame to slab

Right
View of the island bench and the garden beyond. The cantilevered island bench floats over a composite marble floor that runs through to the dining and living areas.

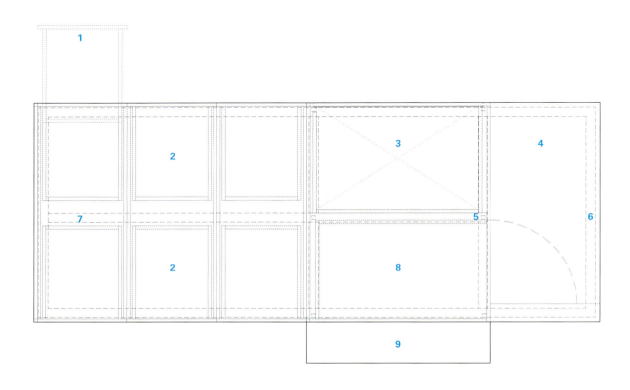

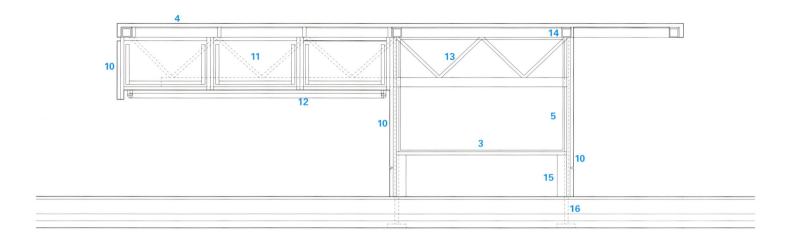

Materials
Worktop DuPont Zodiaq 'Chalk White' composite stone
Joinery Bespoke cabinetry by bespoke.eu
Floor Technical Marble in Special White from Surface, London
Splashback Low iron glass, back painted white, front etched

Appliances and Fixtures
Tap and Spout Hansgrohe Talis S Variarc single lever mixer
Sink Blanco Clarox 500-U
Dishwasher Miele integrated dishwasher
Refrigerator AEG integrated fridge
Freezer Electrolux integrated freezer
Hob Britannia five burner gas hob
Oven Britannia built-in 90cm double oven
Speakers B&W ceiling speakers CCM80
Lighting Kreon

Project Credits
Completion 2007
Client Sally and Simon Nicklin
Structural Engineers Tall Consulting Structural Engineers
Main Contractor Focal Point Construction Ltd
Party Wall Surveyor Martin Lewy

Barton Myers Associates

Rogers Residence
Los Angeles, California, USA

This elegant house is comprised of a group of three buildings positioned around a central courtyard. The three buildings form an ensemble that frames and encloses the intimate central courtyard and lap pool. The courtyard's location, facing south-east, takes full advantage of sunlight and encompasses a sun filled area for the lap pool, a covered and semi-protected patio for year-round outdoor dining and covered porches for lounging and entertaining.

The main building is constructed from an exposed structural steel frame, with a metal deck ceiling and concrete floors. The structures are open, loft-like spaces enclosed by glazed aluminium sectional doors, which can be opened and closed to varying degrees. North-facing clerestory windows provide the exterior elevation with constant, even light. Galvanized rolling shutters above every glazed opening create a secondary envelope that provides additional security, insulation and sun control.

The focal point of the house is the kitchen, which is designed for entertaining. A Caesarstone countertop forms the central kitchen island around which people tend to congregate. Open shelves and translucent glass cabinets provide storage and easy access to frequently used items. Extensive drawers and cabinets are provided to store cooking utensils. A cooking counter with its own sink, range and easy access to the under-counter convection ovens is organized on one side of the kitchen, while the other counter is intended for beverage making and is located next to the coffee machine, refrigerators and a smaller prep-sink.

A butler's pantry with its own sink and dishwasher is located across the hallway from the main kitchen and provides an additional clean-up area so that dirty dishes can be carried away from the centre of the party.

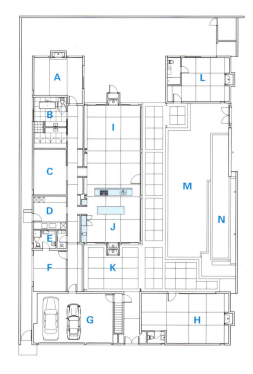

Opposite Left
View of the main living space from the courtyard. A covered area of polished concrete mediates between the structured formality of the house and the informality of the garden where drought-resistant native plants, gravel and boulders create a striking relaxation space.

Floor Plan
 A Master bedroom
 B Bathroom
 C Bedroom
 D Butler's pantry
 E Bathroom
 F Bedroom
 G Garage
 H Games room
 I Living room
 J Kitchen
 K Courtyard
 L Outdoor dining area
M Landscaped courtyard
 N Lap pool

Above Left
The kitchen is comprised of two main elements – the island bench and the cooking counter with overhead storage. Both elements feature 'Ceasarstone' counter tops – a particularly hard wearing engineered stone made up of 94 per cent natural quartz.

Below Left
The kitchen is at the heart of the entertaining area of the house. Guests and residents can take advantage of the kitchen's proximity to both the casual seating and fireplace in the living area, and direct access to the courtyard via expansive sliding glass doors.

Stone

Barton Myers Associates
Rogers Residence
Los Angeles, California, USA

Kitchen Plan and Elevations A and B
1:50
1 Caesarstone countertop
2 Gas hob
3 Line of dishwasher below
4 Stainless steel double sink
5 Shelving and desk
6 Doorway to butler's

pantry
7 Refrigerator
8 Secondary sink
9 Stainless steel countertop and storage units
10 Caesarstone countertop to island bench with built-in ovens under
11 Living area
12 Fireplace

13 Timber shelf
14 Power outlet
15 Timber drawer front
16 Extractor unit
17 Pot filler hose
18 Timber fronted integrated dishwasher
19 Stainless steel spout and taps
20 Translucent glass-fronted cabinets

21 Stainless steel splashback
22 Stainless steel kickplate
23 Open shelves
24 Stainless steel door
25 Stainless steel drawers
26 Stainless steel refrigerator door
27 Stainless steel freezer drawers

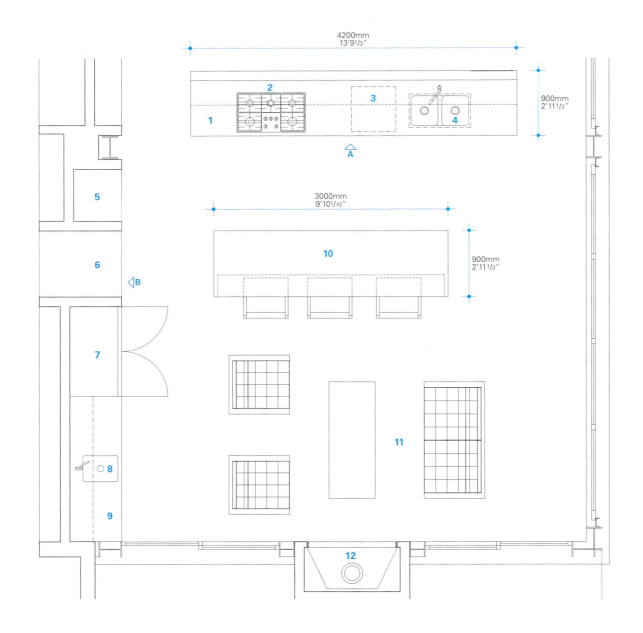

Materials
Worktop Caeserstone and stainless steel
Joinery Poliform / Varenna
Floor Polished cast in situ concrete

Appliances and Fixtures
Taps Franke, model FF–1100
Spout Franke, model FF 600
Sink Franke, model PSX-110-30-9/12
Disposal Unit In-sink-erator, model 777ss
Dishwasher Miele, model Touchtronic Premier Plus
Refrigerator Subzero, model 700TC
Hob Bosch, model KM 342 G-SS
Oven Kuppersbusch, model EEB 9600.
Microwave Maytag
Extractor Miele, model DA259

Project Credits
Completion 2006
Client Richard and Carmen Rogers
Project Architects Barton Myers, Thomas Schneider, Ed Levin, Jorge Narino, Peter Robertson
Structural Engineers Norman J. Epstein
Services Engineer The Sullivan Partnership
Cost Consultant C.P. O'Halloran & Associates
Lighting Consultant Horton Lees Brogden
General Contractor HRB General Contractors

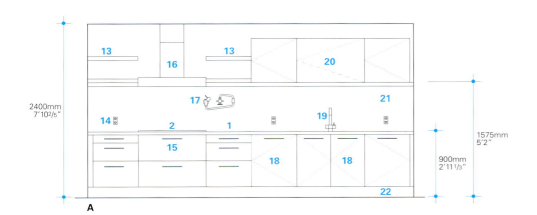

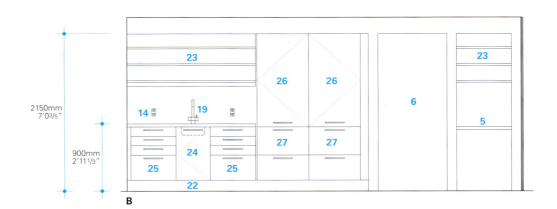

Hudson Architects

Built into the hillside of the Derbyshire countryside, offering spectacular uninterrupted views of the Amber Valley, The Light House is divided into three distinct zones characterized by their materiality. With its northerly side built into the rock of the hill, the building's materiality becomes progressively light towards the south elevation, moving from solid red stone (matching that quarried locally and found on the site), to timber and then glass.

A red stone boundary wall anchors the property into the landscape and runs into the interior, featuring extensively in polished form in the entrance hall. The roof of heavy slate tiles wraps around and down the north-west wall and is punctured only once with a 3.8 metre (12 1/2 feet) diameter opening, allowing light into the central sunken courtyard.

The entrance is via an oak panelled door into the hallway. From here are the open plan kitchen, dining and living areas that together form the focus of the house. The living space is orientated towards a fireplace, drawing the eye to the south-west glazed elevation and the dramatic sun lounge and balconies. The lightness of the south-facing façade culminates in the spectacular two storey sun lounge, which protrudes from the house over the grounds.

The kitchen is characterized by a custom-built double extractor housed in a suspended stainless steel drum, the form of which rhymes with the circular roof opening. Integrated into a storage wall, the kitchen island forms a pastel-hued sculptural backdrop to the room and neatly conceals a wealth of storage. Each side of the island unit has been carefully considered to provide a different function – double fridges and cocktail bar towards the courtyard pool, cooking facilities to the rear side and dining service to the front. The success of the kitchen lies in its effortless mix of practical features and elegant form.

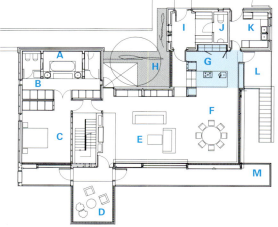

Opposite Left

The house becomes progressively light as it moves away from the solidity at the street side towards the garden, where the façade dissolves into planes of expansive glazing. Notably, a double-height sun lounge cantilevers out over the rolling landscape.

Floor Plan

A Master bathroom
B Dressing room
C Master bedroom
D Sun lounge
E Living room
F Dining room
G Kitchen
H Sunken courtyard and pool
I Entrance
J WC
K Laundry
L Balcony and stair to garden
M Terrace

Left

The kitchen features a large simple island bench with under-bench storage to both sides. To the left, right and behind the bench is additional storage for kitchen equipment and utensils.

Bottom Left

The east wall features a display cabinet of glass shelves and doors placed over a translucent window pane, used to display glassware and ceramics.

Bottom Right

Behind the island bench, a wall of pastel blue storage cupboards is set into the redstone wall. The doors fold out of sight to allow full access to the contents.

Stone

Hudson Architects
The Lighthouse
Derbyshire, England, UK

**Kitchen Plan, Sections
A–A, B–B and Elevation A
1:50**
1 Door to entrance lobby
2 Built-in oven
3 Under-bench storage
4 Dining storage including service trolley
5 Composite stone island bench
6 Gas hob
7 Stainless steel sink
8 Glass display cabinet
9 Rear worktop and enclosed shelving
10 Door to utility room
11 Television
12 Stainless steel spout and taps
13 Painted MDF drawers
14 Overhead storage
15 High storage to entrance

hallway
16 Painted MDF doors on slide and fold track to rear worktop and storage behind
17 Redstone wall behind
18 Fridge and freezer drawers
19 Painted MDF drawers

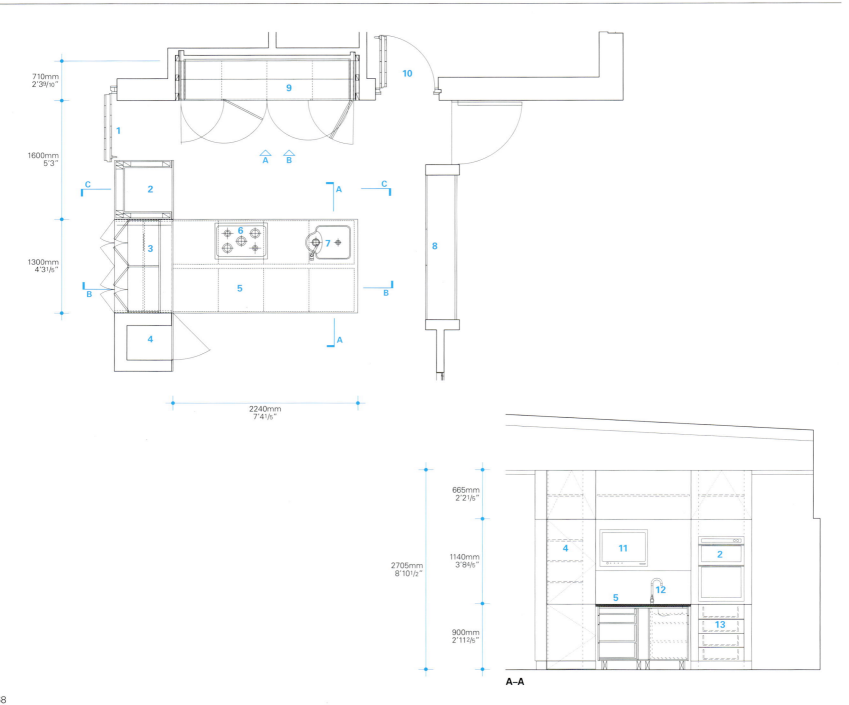

A–A

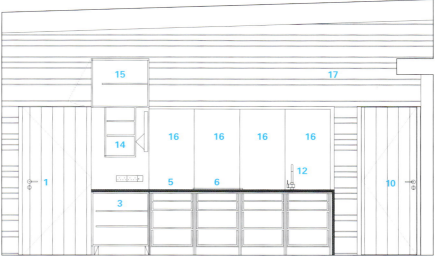

B–B

A

Stone

Hudson Architects
The Lighthouse
Derbyshire, England, UK

Elevation B (Cupboard with Doors Open)
1:20

1 Folding, retractable MDF doors, factory sprayed with two-pack paint
2 Stainless steel support pins for glass shelves
3 Glass shelf
4 Electrical outlets
5 Light switch

6 Composite stone worktop
7 Two-pack sprayed MDF fronts to fridge and freezer drawers
8 Two-pack sprayed MDF drawer fronts
9 Two-pack sprayed MDF kick plate

Section C–C
1:20

1 Line of sink behind
2 Stainless steel spout and tap
3 Two-pack sprayed MDF drawer fronts
4 Gas hob
5 Two-pack sprayed MDF kick plate
6 Overhead storage

cupboard
7 Built-in oven
8 Timber stud wall with painted plasterboard finish

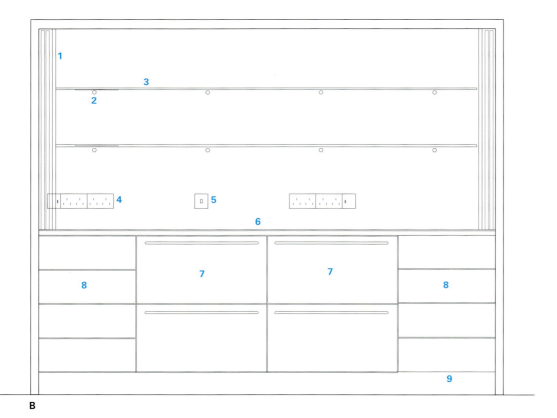

B

Materials
Worktop 25 mm (1 inch) thick Quarella composite stone by PianoForte
Joinery (Floor) 25 mm (1 inch) thick square-edged solid oak with underfloor heating
Tiles 20 mm (3/4 inch) thick Farrer Red Sandstone, sealed finish by Farrer Stone

Appliances and Fixtures
Taps and Spout Abode Hydrus monobloc mixer
Sink Franke undermounted stainless steel sink with integrated waste disposal and vegetable washer
Dishwasher Fischer & Paykel
Refrigerator Subzero
Hob De Dietrich
Oven De Dietrich
Extractor Elica D R Cooker Hoods, bespoke cylindrical case fitted with downlights fabricated by Hayes Industries Ltd
Lighting Lutron controlled lighting system

Project Credits
Completion 2006
Client Jackie Lee
Project Architects Anthony Hudson, Dieter Kleiner
Structural Engineers Techniker
Services Engineer Bridgford Construction
Quantity Surveyor Burke Hunter Adams
Landscape Designer Diarmuid Gavin

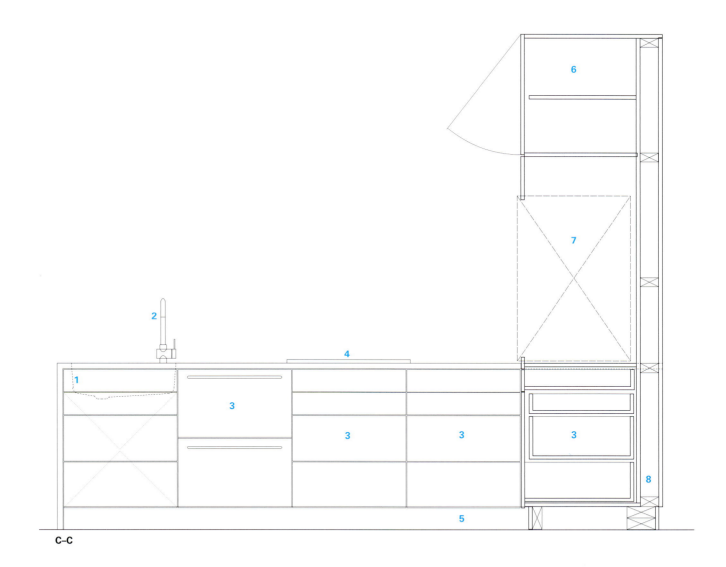

C–C

Timber Kitchens

Tzannes Associates

Mosman Residence
Sydney, New South
Wales, Australia

The Mosman Residence is located on a steep site on Sydney's North Shore. The house is cut into the hillside so that it appears as a single level fronting the road, while at the rear all three levels overlook Balmoral Beach and Middle Harbour.

At street level, the residence maintains a low profile in order to respect existing views of the harbour from residences across the road. This upper level incorporates an undercover entrance with an adjacent courtyard garden, double garage, study and living areas. The north-facing living space dominates this floor and is backlit by south-facing clerestory glazing. The space is accentuated and the view of the harbour is framed by a raked ceiling

that kicks back up over the balcony which runs the full width of the house. Articulated steelwork frames the view and glazed balustrades extend the space.

The kitchen is situated at the end of the open plan top floor. Its proximity to the living and dining areas ensures that the kitchen is at the social heart of the house. The kitchen also maintains a degree of privacy through the high-level island bench upstand, which not only provides storage for the dining area, but also screens the worktop. To maximize bench space, the island returns in an L-shape, with a seating area located at the return end of the bench.

Timber veneer was selected for the

cupboard fronts, with a solid timber finish for the island bench upstand. The timber adds texture and warmth to the grey of the floor and steelwork of the structure. Stone was selected for the island bench worktop, and stainless steel for the main worktop, both durable and aesthetically sophisticated materials.

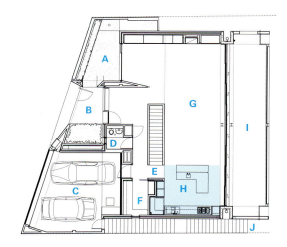

Opposite Left
View from the harbour side of the house where a white-painted steel frame articulates two levels of full-width terraces. Mature gum trees provide welcome shade to the north-facing living spaces.

Floor Plan
A Courtyard garden
B Main entrance
C Garage
D WC
E Stair down lower levels
F Study
G Living and dining areas
H Kitchen
I Terrace
J External stair

Above
Timber veneer to all cupboard and drawer fronts are detailed with simple stainless steel D-handles. Stainless steel and stone worktops lend a cool simplicity to the design.

Below
Fully integrated appliances including the full-height refrigerator and freezer (centre) contribute to the seamless quality of the kitchen.

Timber

Tzannes Associates
Mosman Residence
Sydney, New South Wales,
Australia

**Kitchen Plan
and Elevation A
1:50**

1 Integrated double oven
2 Gas hob
3 Wok burner
4 Stainless steel
   countertop
5 Integrated dishwasher
6 Stainless steel double
   sink

7 Pantry
8 Integrated refrigerator
9 Integrated freezer
10 Sliding glass doors to
   terrace
11 Recess for bench seating
12 Timber veneer under-
   bench cupboards
13 Hot water boiling unit
14 Stainless steel sink
15 Appliance recess

16 Timber veneer high-level
   cupboard fronts
17 Extractor
18 Plate warmer
19 Timber veneer drawer
   fronts
20 Timber veneer high-level
   cupboards with shelving
21 Power outlet
22 Timber veneer kickplate
23 Stainless steel spout and

taps
24 In-sink waste disposal
   unit
25 Pull-out bin

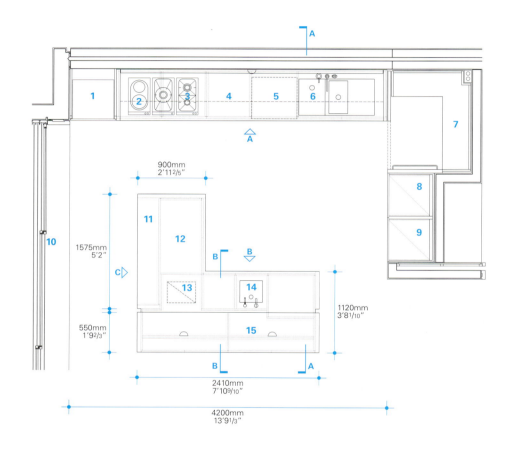

Section A–A
1:20

1 Line of island bench upstand
2 Solid timber island bench upstand countertop
3 Stainless steel spout and taps
4 Stainless steel sink
5 In-sink waste disposal unit
6 Timber veneer drawer fronts
7 Timber veneer kickplate
8 Side panel to island in 50 mm (2 inch) thick stone
9 Stainless steel air-conditioning grille
10 Timber veneer cupboard fronts
11 Concealed under-cupboard lighting
12 Stainless steel worktop

A–A

Timber

Tzannes Associates
Mosman Residence
Sydney, New South Wales,
Australia

**Kitchen Island Bench
Elevation B, Section B–B,
Elevation C
1:20**

1 50 mm (2 inch) solid
   timber top to island
   bench upstand
2 Recessed stone
   splashback
3 50 mm (2 inch) thick
   stone side panel

4 Integrated dishwasher
   with timber veneer front
5 Stainless steel power
   outlet
6 Hot water tap
7 Mixer tap
8 Integrated stone sink
9 In-sink waste disposal
10 Timber veneer drawer
   fronts
11 Timber kickplate

12 50 mm (2 inch) thick
   stone side panel with
   joinery beyond
13 50 mm (2 inch) thick
   stone worktop
14 Island bench upstand
   cupboard doors in timber
   veneer
15 Shelves to dining room
16 Hot water boiling unit

Right
View of the kitchen from the
living area. Full-height glazing
slides away to open up the
spaces to the spectacular
view. At the end of the
terrace, adjacent to the
kitchen, a BBQ creates the
opportunity for outdoor
cooking and dining.

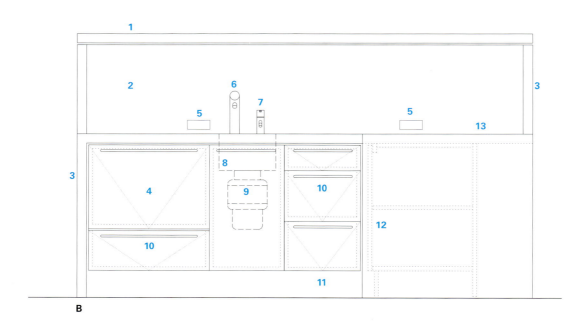

B

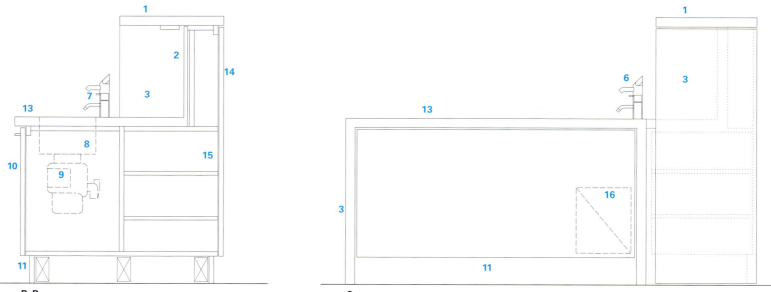

B–B

C

78

Materials
Worktop Caesarstone Quartz Finish 'Ice Snow'
Joinery Timber veneer of Australian Spotted Gum,
quarter cut
Floor Pietra di Bedonia 300 x 600 mm (114/5 x 233/4 inch) tiles

Appliances and Fixtures
Taps Vola KV1 Kitchen Tap
Disposal Unit In-Sink-Erator M65 with Hafele bin pull outs
Dishwasher Miele G 896 Sci Plus integrated dishwasher
Refrigerator Liebherr SBS 5712 side by side fridge
Hob Gaggenau VG232 2 burner and VG 231 wok burner
Oven Gaggenau EB261-130
Steam Oven Gaggenau ED220-100
Plate Warmer Gaggenau
Microwave Panasonic NN T791SF
Extractor Qasair UV1000-2

Project Credits
Completion 2005
Project Architects Alec Tzannes, Phillip Rossington, Sally
Edwards, Imogene Potter
Structural Engineers Simpsor Design
Main Contractor Ant Building
Hydraulic Consultant Whipps Wood consulting
Landscape Consultant Michael Phillips

Jamie Fobert Architects Kander House
London, England, UK

The Kander House is a reconfigured Victorian townhouse in North London. Its existing unsound structural condition focussed the architect's attention, presenting an opportunity to reconsider the habitats of a typical Victorian home from first principles.

In consideration of the existing site conditions and the client's desire for generous volumes to accommodate family life, a distinctive and sculptural concrete structure was designed for the lower floors – a compelling object in its own right which also acts as vital structural support for the building.

The kitchen is arranged as an open plan area on the ground floor which addresses the main living space and gives views to the terrace and garden beyond. The kitchen is comprised of two principal objects: a linear run of full-height timber units, comprising storage and a recessed counter, and a stainless steel island unit, providing further low-level storage and housing gas hob rings and an additional preparation sink.

The kitchen is constructed using only two materials. The primary material is Stia, a German-engineered multi-ply board constructed from layers of oak sandwiched between balancing layers with an oak finish to both faces which has alternating strips of oak. The second material, stainless steel, is used for all of the countertops and the island unit.

The island unit is fabricated entirely in stainless steel using 10 millimetre (2/5 inch) thick solid plates for the top counter surface and return faces. The gas hob rings are mounted directly onto the counter with no surrounding plate in order to create a single uninterrupted surface, and the under-mounted stainless steel sink is welded directly to the underside of the counter and polished smooth to help the island to read as a singular sculptural object.

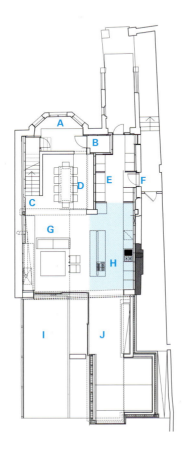

Opposite Left
A stainless steel island bench provides an elegant transition between the open kitchen and the dining and living spaces. A full height timber wall standing on a recessed plinth appears to float against the double-height wall.

Opposite Centre
Beyond the kitchen, towards the front of the house, a wall-mounted timber sideboard provides a focus for the dining area as well as creating extra storage.

Floor Plan
 A Study
 B WC
 C Stair to first floor
 D Dining area
 E Pantry
 F Side entrance
 G Living area
 H Kitchen
 I Garden terrace
 J Terrace

Left
The ground floor kitchen occupies a dramatic double-height space which connects the street entrance at an upper level with the garden at the rear in one continuous space. New unpainted shuttered concrete walls denote the new architectural interventions in this Victorian house and provide a contemporary environment for the clean lines of the stainless steel island and full-height timber storage wall of the kitchen.

Timber

Jamie Fobert Architects
Kander House
London, England, UK

**Kitchen Plan, Elevations
A, B and C, Sections A–A,
B–B and C–C
1:50**

1 Double sink
2 Dishwasher below
3 Stainless steel countertop
4 Gas hob
5 Metal stud wall
6 Timber-faced cupboards
   with shelving behind
7 Side table
8 Timber-faced joinery unit
9 Concrete column
10 Stainless steel inset sink
11 Stainless steel island unit
12 Counter mounted gas hob units
13 Stainless steel splashback
14 Mixer tap
15 Integrated dishwasher
16 Timber-faced drawer unit
17 Stainless steel shelf
18 Concealed extractor unit
19 Integrated fridge-freezer
20 Stainless steel light fitting
21 Microwave
22 Pull-out shelving units
23 Pull-out pantry shelving
24 Under-shelf lighting
25 Concealed extractor unit

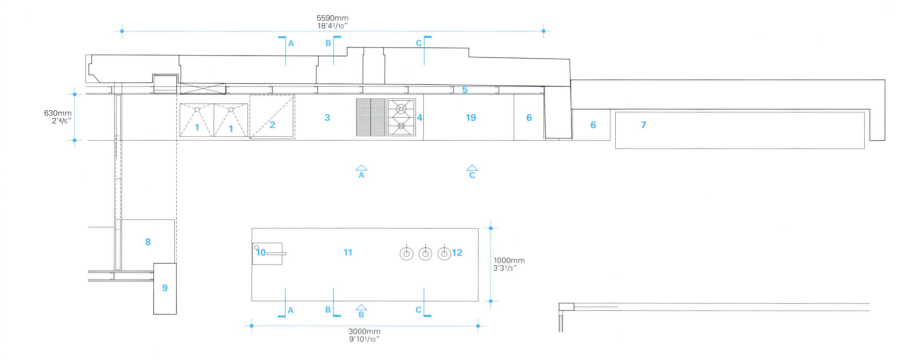

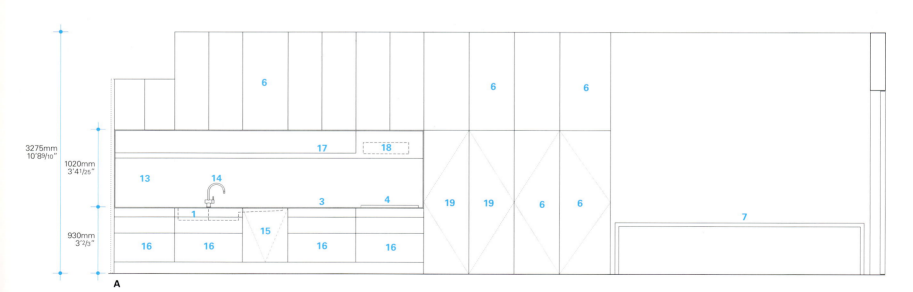

Materials
Worktop 10 mm (2/5 inch) stainless steel plate
Joinery 19 mm (3/4 inch) Stia oak panels
Floor Power-floated polished concrete

Appliances and Fixtures
Taps Chrome KWC single mixer tap
Spout Chrome KWC single mixer spout
Sink Stainless steel bespoke unit
Hob Gaggenau
Oven Gaggenau
Lighting Stainless steel bespoke fitting with S12 lamps and under-mounted shelf fittings with S12 lamps

Project Credits
Completion 2004
Client Nicole and Nadav Kander
Project Architects Kevin Allsop, Liza Thomson-Farrell, Michael Gollings, Pierre Maré, Hoi Chi Ng, Emily Roberts, Tessa Schaap
Structural Engineers Elliott Wood Partnership
Services Engineer Mendick Waring
Quantity Surveyor Measur

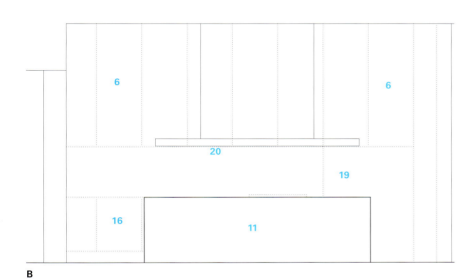

B

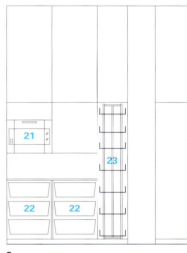

C

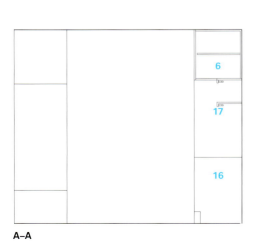

A–A

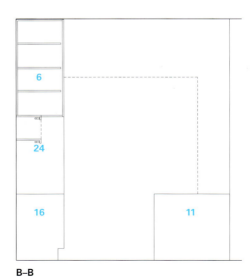

B–B

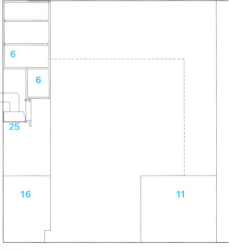

C–C

Huttunen-Lipasti Architects

Päivärinne House
Salo, Varsinais-Suomi, Finland

This simple family house is situated in an existing apple orchard in the southern Finnish countryside, where it stands between a small country road and a sloping landscape of fields. The two storey timber house with its façade treated with a mixture of tar and oil, accommodates the main living spaces, an office, utility room, WC and garage on the ground level while on the first floor are bedrooms, the bathroom and a sauna. All of the spaces open up to views of the landscape to the south.

The kitchen is located at the centre of the ground floor and functions as the heart and soul of the main living areas. Consisting of a wall of white floor and wall-mounted cupboards with a stainless steel countertop, and an island unit with a timber countertop, the kitchen overlooks the main living spaces and has direct access to a timber-decked terrace that runs the full length of the house and overlooks the orchard.

The deliberately simple and neutral kitchen was designed with as few details as possible. The structural system for the joinery is plywood covered with melamine with doors made of painted MDF. Almost all of the surfaces are painted matt white – only the worktop and counter are treated differently. The worktop is of wax-treated ash and the counter is brushed stainless steel. Exposed edges are expressed as 20 millimetre (3/4 inch)

thick sections, despite the comparative slenderness of the material.

On the back wall behind the counter a ceramic artwork is planned which will lend an extra element of drama to the calm space, framed by the simple white doors.

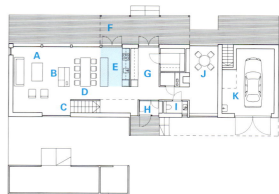

Opposite Left
The two storey timber house sits in an idyllic country setting which includes an existing apple orchard.

Floor Plan
A Living room
B Fireplace
C Stair to first floor
D Dining area
E Kitchen
F Terrace
G Laundry and utility room
H Closet
 I WC
J Office
K Garage

Left
The kitchen enjoys calming views out over the orchard with direct access to the garden via a partly covered terrace.

Below Left
The whole of the interior is characterized by white walls with accents of warm timber. This palette is echoed in the kitchen, where a wall of white cupboards contains the bulk of the storage while a timber topped island bench mediates between the kitchen and the dining area.

Timber

Huttunen-Lipasti Architects
Päivärinne House
Salo, Varsinais-Suomi,
Finland

Kitchen Plan and Section A–A
1:50
1 Covered terrace
2 Laundry and utility room storage cupboard
3 Hob
4 Stainless steel countertop
5 Stainless steel sink
6 Integrated refrigerator
7 Timber island bench
8 Dining area
9 Fireplace
10 Stair to first floor
11 Full-height glazed doors
12 White-painted MDF cupboard doors
13 Oven
14 Stainless steel tap
15 Hallway to laundry and study

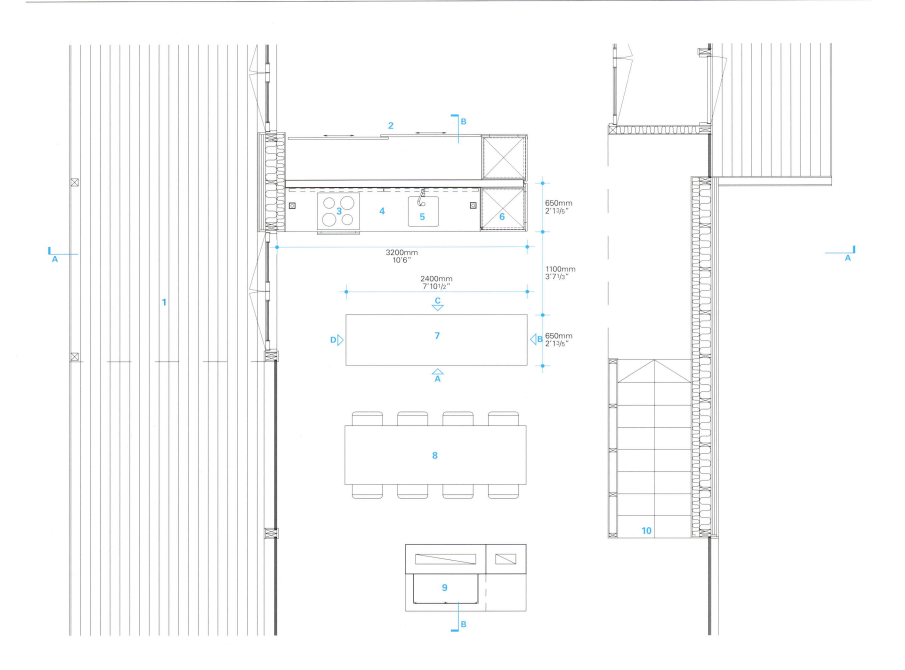

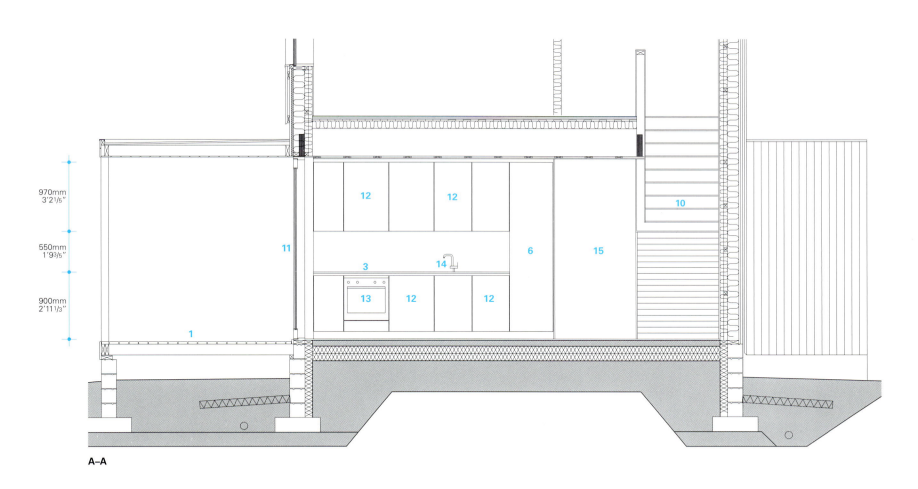

970mm
3'2¹/₅"

550mm
1'9³/₅"

900mm
2'11¹/₃"

1

11

3

14

13

12

12

12

12

6

15

10

A–A

Timber

Huttunen-Lipasti Architects
Päivärinne House
Salo, Varsinais-Suomi,
Finland

Section B–B and Island Unit
Elevations A, B, C and D
1:50
1 Timber countertop to island bench
2 Painted MDF drawers to island unit
3 Full-height glazed doors to terrace
4 Painted MDF wall-
mounted cupboards
5 Stainless steel tap and spout
6 Stainless steel sink
7 Painted MDF drawers
8 Cupboards to utility room
9 Painted MDF front to island unit
10 Painted MDF side to island unit
11 Stainless steel shadow
line below countertop
12 Painted MDF side to island unit with power points

Right
The kitchen acts as both a neutral backdrop to the living spaces and the hub of family life. A large fireplace separates the dining and living areas.

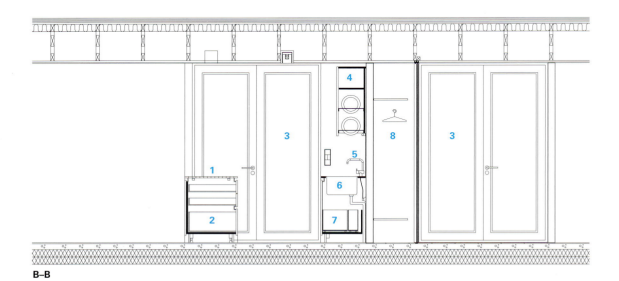

B–B

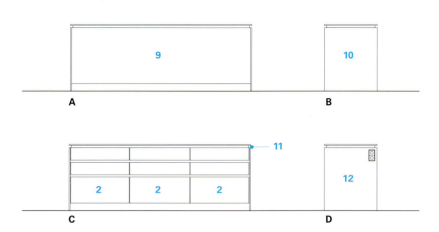

Materials
Worktop Wax-treated ash and stainless steel
Joinery Melamine-covered plywood with painted MDF doors and aluminium extruded section to under-counter shadow line
Floor Ash parquetry

Appliances and Fixtures
Taps and Spout Vola, designed by Arne Jacobsen
Sink Francke stainless steel integrated under counter sink
Disposal Unit Stala Ecoline
Dishwasher Siemens SL65T371EU
Refrigerator Siemens K138RA40
Oven Siemens HB430510S
Microwave Siemens HF17025EU
Extractor Siemens LB 54564SD
Lighting Deltalight Limit ZB and minigrid in Limit ZB and pendant light A440 by Artek over dining table

Project Credits
Completion 2006
Project Architects Santeri Lipasti
Structural Engineers Jukka Toivonen
Services Engineer Markku Kallio
Quantity Surveyor Tero Lehtonen
Kitchen Manufacturer Arttelipuu

Marsh Cashman Koolloos Architects

The White House Sydney, New South Wales, Australia

The White House is a handsomely restored Federation house with a typical palette of sandstone, shingles and face-brick, all of which were continued in the new work. The clients needed a family home with open, flowing spaces that connected garden, pool and the interior – a contemporary refurbishment that respected the old house.

An addition to the rear is designed conceptually as a hand that gently grabs the old house and engages with it directly and sympathetically. The external façade of the old house stands proud in the new double-height living room, creating an ambiguity between internal and external space. This atmosphere is reinforced when the glass sliding doors that separate the room from the garden disappear into a large steel box concealing them from view so that space flows and extends horizontally and vertically.

The contemporary, abstract interior features an enigmatic floating box cantilevering out into the double-height void. When the doors are stacked away in their steel box home, the movement is seamless and uninterrupted. The rear façade to the old house is, in fact, sitting in the new living room, with the complete façade with gable and chimney on display.

The kitchen is seamlessly integrated into the concrete and timber interior – echoing both the materials and monolithic nature of the main living space. A wall of recycled timber cupboards are layered against the wall, blending with walls, splashback and ceiling of the same material. The robustly-scaled island unit is constructed from in situ concrete and, with its seating rebate, forms a natural social focus for the living space.

Opposite Left

View from the decked pool area which can be viewed directly from the kitchen.

Opposite Centre

View from the kitchen out towards the pool. Recycled hardwood features throughout the ground floor, in the flooring, exposed ceiling beams and the kitchen joinery.

Floor Plan

A Entrance
B Verandah
C Living room 1
D Hallway
E Study / office
F WC
G Laundry
H Pantry
I Living room 2
J Kitchen
K Glazed wall
L Pool room
M Garden
N Pool

Above

The existing brick façade is evident in the new double-height living space where it now creates a textured backdrop to the predominantly white and neutral-hued palette. The kitchen (right) features full-height timber joinery and a simple island bench to create the transition between kitchen and living room.

Below

A feature wall of reclaimed hardwood anchors the kitchen to the frame of the house. High-level cupboards of the same material provide high-level storage while large appliances (refrigerator and ovens) are integrated into the joinery. A cast in situ concrete island bench provides a welcome counterpoint to the warmth of the timber.

**Marsh Cashman Koolloos
Architects**
The White House
Sydney, New South Wales,
Australia

**Kitchen Plan, Elevation A
and Section A–A
1:50**
1 Line of under-bench
   rebate for seating
2 Stainless steel sink
3 Concrete island worktop
4 Cast concrete worktop
5 Gas hob
6 Full height joinery with
   integrated oven and
   microwave
7 Stainless steel fridge-
   freezer
8 Pantry
9 Pantry prep sink
10 Cavity screen door
11 Laundry
12 Exposed ceiling rafters
13 Timber-faced overhead
   cupboards
14 Timber-faced tall storage
   cupboard
15 Microwave
16 Oven
17 Timber-faced drawers
18 Concealed exhaust unit
19 Timber splashback
20 Pot storage drawers
21 Under-bench storage
   cupboard
22 Fascia to concrete
   worktop
23 Mixer tap

**Island Counter Plan and
Elevations B and
Section B–B
1:50**
1 Concrete support wall to
   island unit
2 Under-bench
   rebate for seating
3 Under-bench storage
   drawers
4 Under-sink cupboard
5 Dishwasher
6 Storage drawers
7 Fascia to concrete
   worktop
8 Mixer tap
9 Concrete island worktop

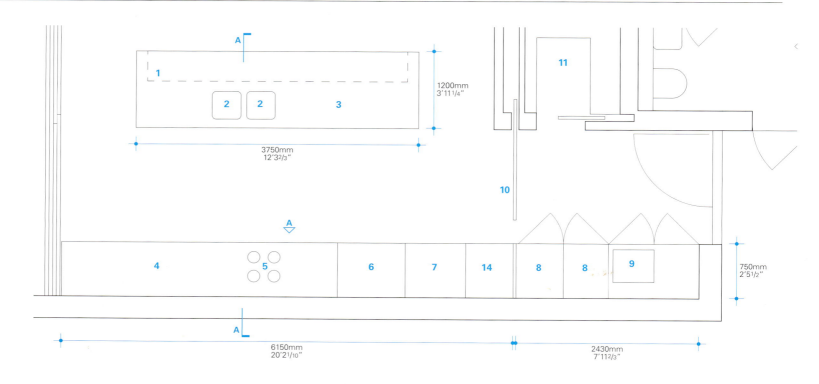

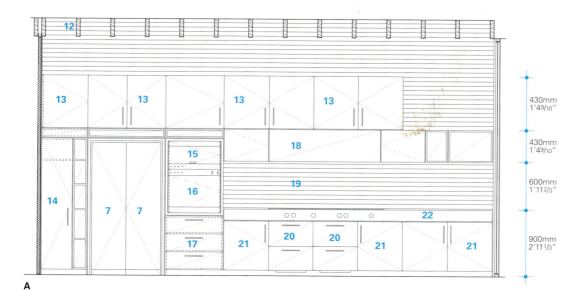

Materials
Worktop Steel trowel finished concrete topping to island and recycled Ironbark timber boards to wall unit
Joinery Solid recycled Ironbark timber boards
Floor Solid recycled Ironbark timber boards

Appliances and Fixtures
Taps and Spout Vola KV1 mixer tap
Sink Stainless steel double sink by Abbey
Dishwasher Fischer + Paykel
Refrigerator Jennair
Hob Gaggenau VG353
Oven Gaggenau EB965-110
Microwave Gaggenau ER 918-011
Extractor Qasair integrated UV1500-3B
Lighting Concealed dimmable T5 fluroescent battens and recessed wall lights by Mondoluce

Project Credits
Completion 2003
Client Peto and Julie White
Project Architects Mark Cashman, Steve Koolloos, Rowena Marsh, Michael Bucherer, Stuart Murchison
Structural Engineers Barry Smith Bateman
Hydraulic Engineer John Amey Associates
Quantity Surveyor BDA Consultants
Landscape Architect Barbara Schaffer
Builder JPA Constructions

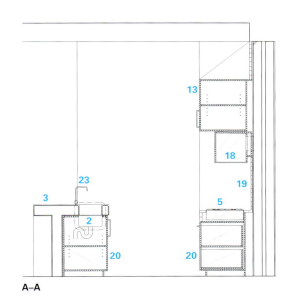

A–A

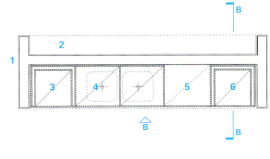

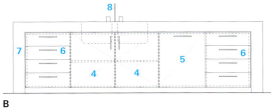

B

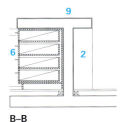

B–B

Niall McLaughlin Architects

House at Dirk Cove Clonakilty, County Cork, Ireland

This old stone cottage, a former coastguard station located on the rock-bound, stormy Atlantic coast of Ireland, has been converted, along with its boatshed, and extended to create a contemporary family home. An asymmetric, cruciform cloister links the components which are built around a small courtyard.

The living space stretches out towards the water and away from the growing shadow of the hill and the new living room is shaped to capture light. The organization of the house is based on a journey towards a view of the horizon. The driveway is screened from the sea and the entrance is via a small courtyard. When the front door is opened a glazed passage reveals a table, beyond which a window frames a view of a distant beach across the bay. Towards the table, two new spaces open up. One is the main living space overlooking the sea. The other is the view out towards the ocean.

The old cottage has been transformed into a master bedroom and the boathouse into guest bedrooms. The kitchen, dining and living rooms occupy the new extension. The new extension projects beyond the sea wall, reaching ten metres (33 feet) out towards the water.

The kitchen sits at the edge of a free-standing pod, which also houses a utility room and WC. The pod is made of factory-sprayed MDF, and the countertops are white polished concrete. The kitchen is part of the main living space, following the angled lines of the extension. The brief asked for a large living space that maximizes views and lets in as much light as possible. With this in mind, the kitchen is an integral and yet understated part of the primary living spaces.

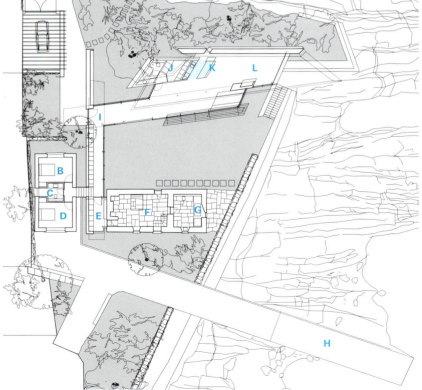

Opposite Left
The new pavilion frames a new courtyard on a site characterized by shards of metamorphic rock that finger out to the sea from the base of the small cliffs.

Floor Plan
A Garage
B Guest bedroom
C Guest bathroom
D Guest bedroom
E Link building / storage
F Master bedroom
G Master bathroom
H Jetty
I Entrance
J Kitchen
K Dining area
L Living area

Above
In the new extension, a primarily open plan, glass-clad space, the kitchen, utility room and WC occupy a white 'pod' whose angled walls echo those of the pavilion itself.

Left
Opposite the kitchen, looking out over the bay through a wall of full-height glass, a custom made white concrete table and bench (left) and timber bench (right) take full advantage of the spectacular views.

Timber

Niall McLaughlin Architects
House at Dirk Cove
Clonakilty, County Cork,
Ireland

**Kitchen Plan and Elevations A and B
1:50**
1 Wall hung WC
2 Basin
3 Lobby to cloakroom and
   utility room
4 Refrigerator
5 Freezer
6 Washing machine
7 Laundry storage
8 Hob with oven under
9 Polished concrete
   worktop
10 Double sink
11 Cupboards
12 Drawers
13 Microwave behind doors
14 Door to utility room and
   WC
15 Overhead cupboards
16 Wall and ceiling structure
to kitchen 'pod'
17 Dishwasher
18 Backlit translucent glass
   splashback
19 Fixed painted MDF
   panels

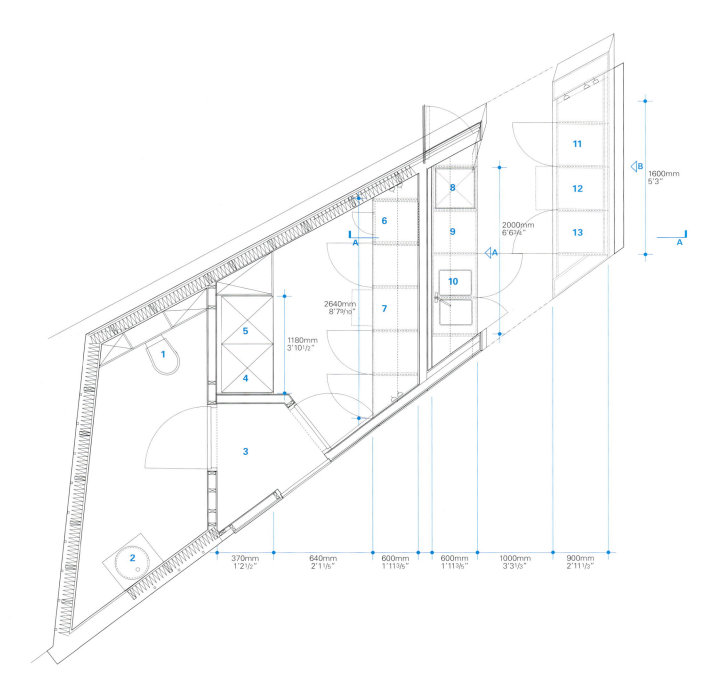

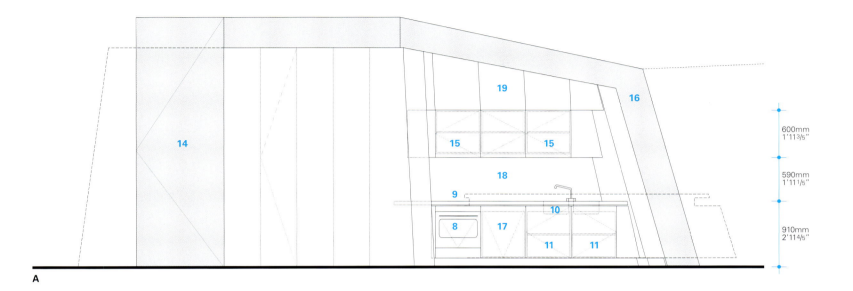

A

19

15   15

18

9

10

8   17

11   11

14

16

600mm
1'11³/₅"

590mm
1'11¹/₅"

910mm
2'11⁴/₅"

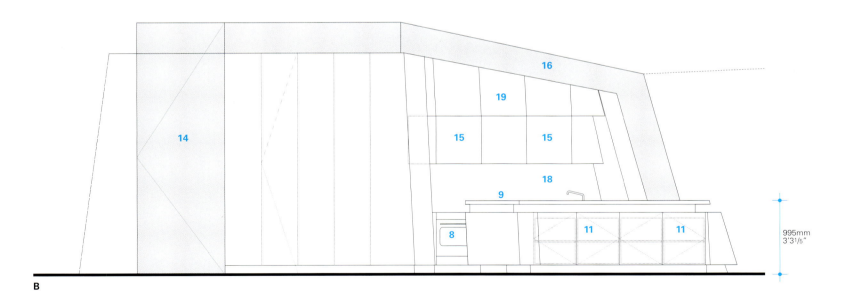

B

16

19

15   15

18

9

8

11   11

14

995mm
3'3¹/₅"

Timber

Niall McLaughlin Architects
House at Dirk Cove
Clonakilty, County Cork,
Ireland

**Kitchen Section A–A
1:20**
1 Roof
2 Window over utility pod
3 Painted plasterboard
   ceiling
4 Painted MDF cupboard
   doors
5 Polished white concrete
   worktop
6 Sprayed MDF kickplate
7 Timber stud wall
8 Concealed fluorescent
   light fitting
9 Fixed painted MDF panel
10 Backlit translucent glass
   splashback
11 Line of fixed panel to pod
   shell
12 Concealed lighting
   behind laminated glass
13 Painted MDF

centreboard between
diaphragms
14 Concealed lighting at
   skirting

**Concrete Table and Bench
Plan 1:50, Elevation A and
Section A–A
1:20**
1 TV and fireplace alcove
2 White concrete bench
3 Mesh table support
4 Welded frame and
   sprayed MDF cover
   panels to table support
5 Line of table supports
6 Window overlooking bay
7 Timber bench
8 Full-height window
9 Outdoor timber bench
10 White concrete tabletop
11 Sprayed MDF cover

panels to table support
12 Welded steel frame
13 Table support screw fixed
   to concrete screed floor
14 Concrete floor

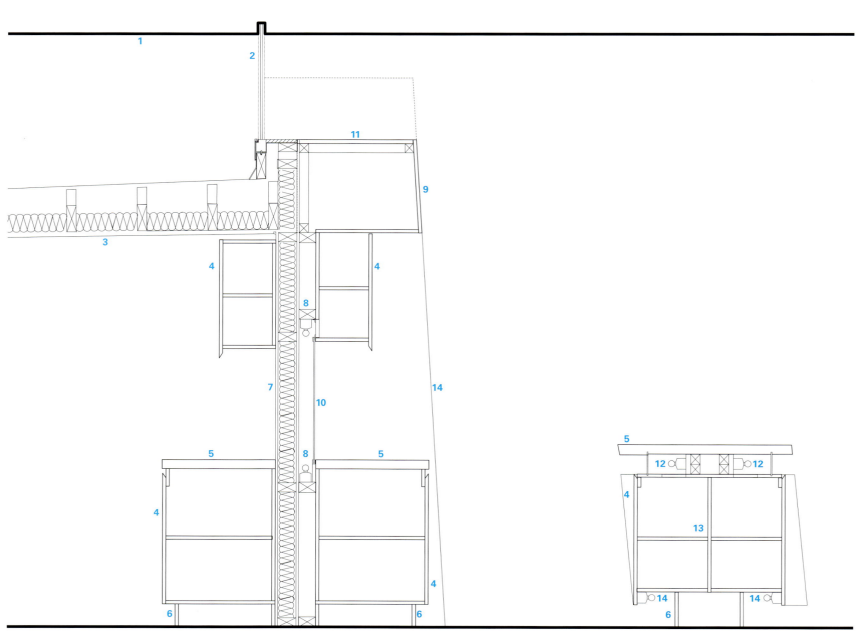

A–A

98

Materials
Worktop White polished concrete
Joinery Bespoke factory-sprayed MDF
Floor White polished concrete

Project Credits
Completion 2004
Project Architects Niall McLaughlin, Spencer Guy
Structural Engineers Packman Lucas
Contract Manager Stephen Jeffrey, The County
Homesearch Company

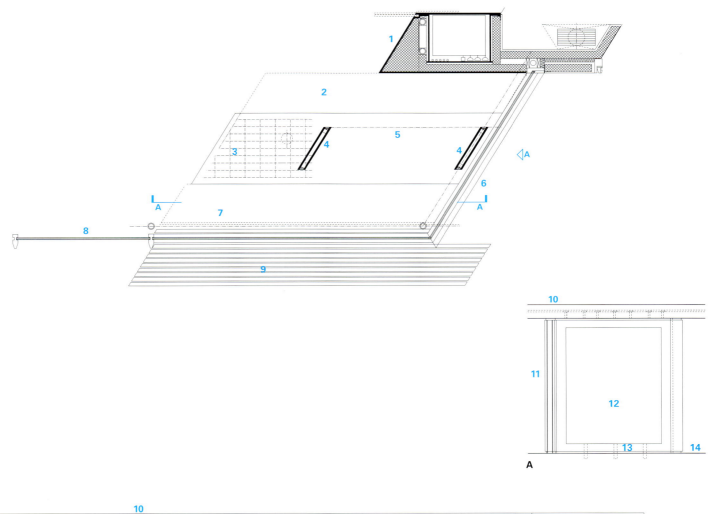

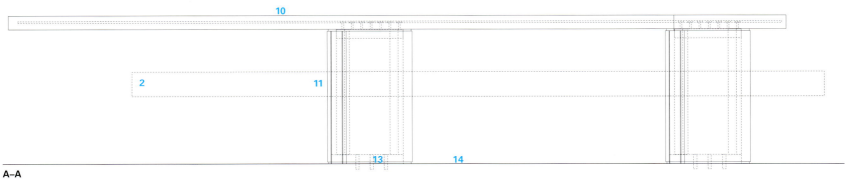

A–A

Scape Architects

1 Perren Street
London, England, UK

Commissioned as a private development for a British documentary maker, 1 Perren Street is a significant new London town house in Kentish Town, North London. Originally an Organ Works, there is little that remains of its previous use in its new incarnation as a spacious five-bedroom house.

With minimal interventions to the façade, the project involved the remodelling of the interior to create a series of connected spaces and playful structural forms around a central stair. Guests arrive in a spacious entrance hall at ground level where private bedrooms are carved out of solid timber cladding.

A timber stair climbs towards the lighter, open plan reception spaces of the upper floor, providing access to the social heart of the house. The kitchen is arranged as a large open L-shape opening up to the dining area. A bespoke Corian countertop is interrupted only by a stainless steel spout and a ceramic hob, while larch-clad cupboard and drawer fronts continue into the living space. A white Corian splashback and white-sprayed high-level cupboards match the existing white sash windows.

Visible from the kitchen and dining area, a six metre (20 foot) high translucent textured GRP (glass reinforced plastic) stair wall rises from the first floor to a frameless glass skylight two stories above, inviting guests upwards to the roof terrace.

On the top floor the stair wall rhymes with a sculptural bath in the master bedroom suite, which is cast in the same material. A restrained palette of warm natural materials is employed throughout: larch wood and phenolic-faced plywood and cork / rubber, with lighting fixtures embedded within the sculptural furniture components to further emphasize material warmth, movement and perspective depth.

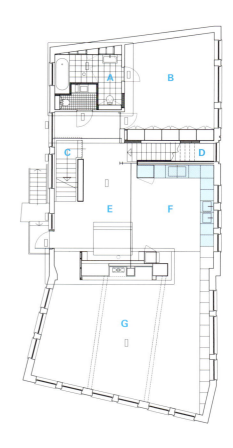

Opposite Left
The building has been transformed from its original incarnation as an organ factory, then as low rent office space, and finally to a handsome family home.

Opposite Centre
Larch wood features throughout the house, including here in the kitchen where the counter continues in a low run of cupboards into the living room.

Floor Plan
A Bathroom
B Bedroom
C Stair to upper floor
D Stair from ground floor
E Dining room
F Kitchen
G Living room

Left
The kitchen opens up in a continuous space that includes the dining area with its custom made dining table which sits next to timber-lined banquette seating.

Below Left
The worktop is made from a continuous slab of white Corian with an integrated double sink. The glass reinforced plastic stair wall with integrated lighting (left) rises through the three levels of the house.

Timber

Scape Architects
1 Perren Street
London, England, UK

**Kitchen Plan
and Elevations A and B
1:50**

1 Integrated refrigerator and freezer
2 Line of high-level cupboards over
3 Ceramic hob set flush in countertop
4 Corian countertop on plywood substrate
5 Bespoke Corian drainer integrated in countertop
6 Bespoke Corian double sink integrated in countertop
7 White lacquered MDF cupboard fronts with continuous concealed fluorescent lighting
8 White Corian splashback
9 Integrated dishwasher
10 Stainless steel spout and taps
11 Larch veneer on plywood cupboard doors
12 Larch veneer on plywood drawer fronts
13 Existing timber sash window frames
14 Larch veneer on plywood cupboard doors with white melamine carcass
behind
15 Integrated oven

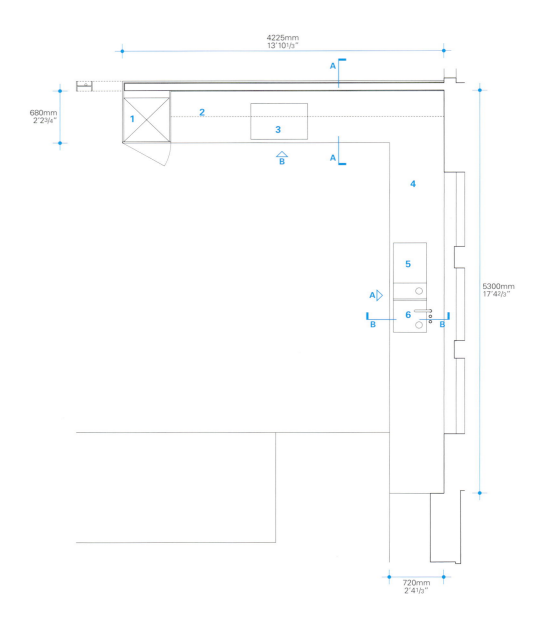

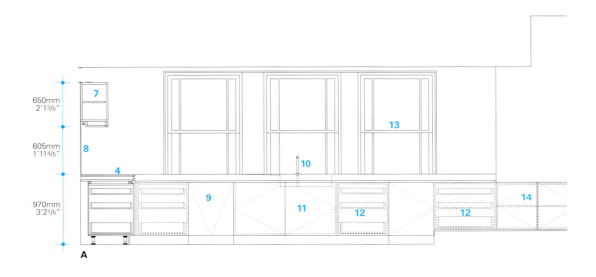

650mm
2'1³/₅"

605mm
1'11⁴/₅"

970mm
3'2¹/₅"

7

8

4

9

10

11

12

13

14

A

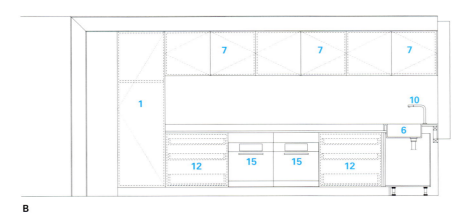

1

7

7

7

10

6

12

15

15

12

B

Timber

Scape Architects
1 Perren Street
London, England, UK

Sections A–A and B–B
1:10
1 Exposed steel beam
2 Insulated timber stud wall
3 Flat duct for kitchen extractor
4 Melamine cupboard carcass
5 Timber batten fixing
6 White sprayed MDF

cupboard door
7 Continuous concealed fluorescent lighting pelmet
8 White Corian splashback
9 Corian countertop on marine plywood substrate
10 Ceramic hob set flush in countertop
11 Aluminium angle forming

recessed finger pull handle
12 Larch faced multiply cupboard doors on white melamine-faced birch ply carcass
13 Drawer
14 Adjustable feet
15 Black melamine-faced MDF kick plate
16 Rubber and cork sheet

flooring
17 Corian edge to sink
18 Bespoke Corian double sink and drainer on marine ply substrate
19 Stainless steel spout and tap
20 Corian backing into existing window frame
21 Service void
22 Sink drain outlet

Right
View from the kitchen towards the living room. A stainless steel-clad fireplace with birch shelves (right) forms a visual transition between the two spaces.

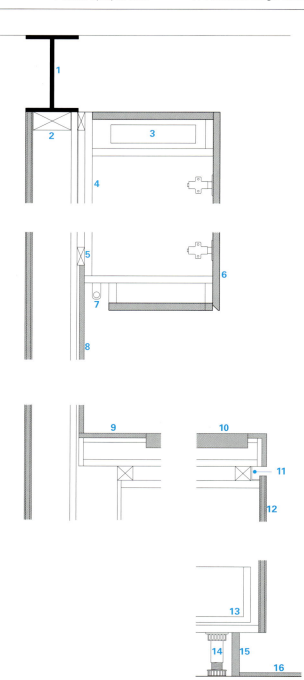

A–A

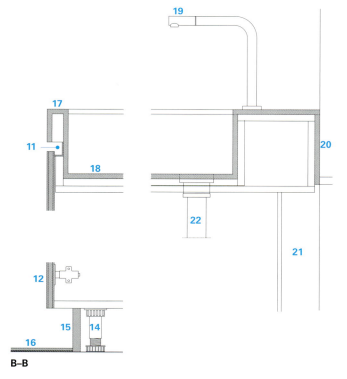

B–B

Materials
Worktop Corian solid surfacing in Bone colour
Splashback Corian solid surfacing colour
Joinery Larch faced plywood doors on melamine-faced birch plywood carcasses
Floor Cork / rubber sheet

Appliances and Fixtures
Taps Binova EGG8
Sink Bespoke Corian sink integrated with worktop
Disposal Unit Insinkerator 65
Dishwasher Miele G 1180 Vi
Refrigerator Miele K855iD- 1
Freezer Meile FG23 Ui-2
Hob Miele KM 552induction hob
Oven Miele H 4680 BP KAT
Extractor Elica BIUHS
Lighting T5 fluorescent strip lighting

Project Credits
Completion 2006
Project Architects Chris Godfrey, Anya Wilson, Pieter Kleinmann, Tracy Mealiff, Ingrid Frydenbo-Bruvoll
Lighting Consultant Dan Heap Ltd
Main Contractor Turner Castle
Specialist Joinery Tin Tab
GRP Fabrications Design and Display Ltd

Turner Castle

Opal House
London, England, UK

When the client was looking to commission an architect for his new house in London, he appointed the architects of his former apartment who had developed an excellent understanding of their client's requirements.

The property is a four storey semi-detached Victorian town house which has been stripped back to its load bearing walls and completely remodelled inside. Externally, the original brickwork and window surrounds have been retained and a modern glazed pavilion has been added to the rear. The real transformation is an assembly of spacious volumes carved out of the original architecture.

At the front of the house, a cantilevered timber and glass open-tread staircase rises through a stupendous triple-height volume. The main entertaining space – living room, dining area and kitchen – is a double-height space with polished concrete floor, that runs the full length of the extended lower ground floor.

The kitchen consists of an island bench with a stainless steel worktop and timber-fronted cupboards and drawers. Running along the perimeter wall, opposite the island bench, is a run of cupboards which give access to a pantry and feature panels of translucent acrylic back-lit 'Opal' panels which lend the house its name.

Throughout the house, a palette of muted neutral colours (pinks, greys and browns) and rich natural materials was chosen to heighten the flow of interconnected spaces. The study shelving and cupboards, stair treads and kitchen island are all finished in dark oak, which is used for the flooring throughout. Colour, shape and texture are added with specially selected and bespoke furniture as well as the client's collection of paintings, books and artefacts.

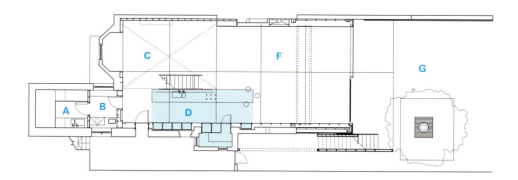

Opposite Left
The original brick façade and windows of the Victorian house were restored, while a glass and steel extension to the ground floor give an indication that the interior of the house has been entirely remodelled.

Floor Plan
A Utility room
B Cloakroom
C Dining room
D Kitchen
E Pantry
F Living room
G Garden

Left
The kitchen features a monolithic island bench with a stainless steel countertop with integrated double sink and gas hob. The side wall of the house has been lined out with a run of full-height cupboards which conceal appliances and pantry storage.

Bottom Left
The island bench extends into a cantilevered bench as it reaches towards the living room. The space terminates in a massive steel-framed glass door which slides open to give access to the garden. The cupboards along the wall give way to back-lit glass panels.

Timber

Turner Castle
Opal House
London, England, UK

Kitchen Plan and Elevation A
1:50
1 Stair to first floor
2 Cupboard carcass with sink above
3 Carcass with oven below and hob above
4 Breakfast bar
5 Spray-painted MDF cupboard doors
6 Built-in refrigerator, dishwasher and microwave
7 Pantry
8 Translucent acrylic Opal panel velcro-fixed to metal studs with fluorescent lights behind
9 Stained oak cupboard fronts
10 Chrome spout and taps
11 Stained oak drawer and cupboard fronts with resin-bonded ply shelves
12 Gas rings
13 Oven

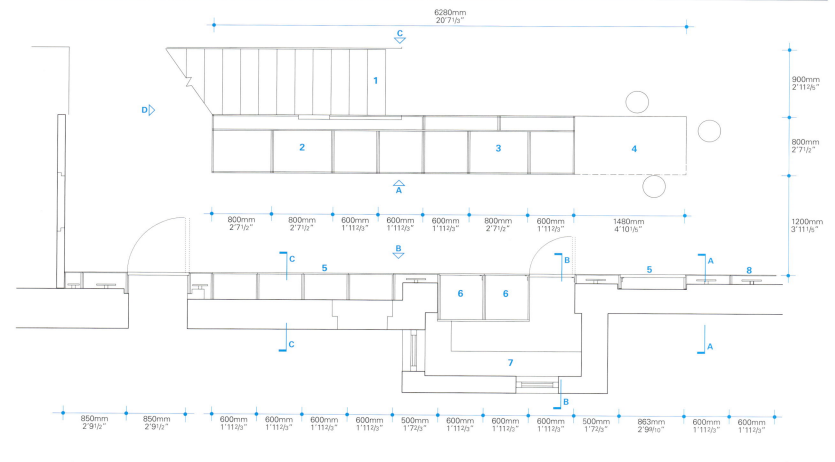

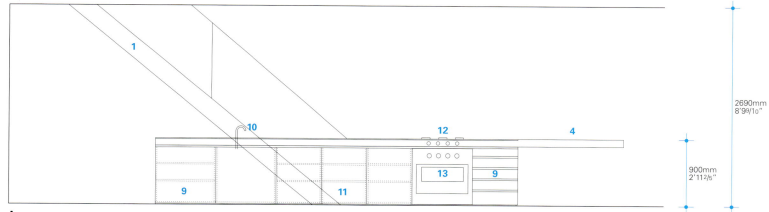

108

**Kitchen Elevation B
1:100**
1 Stair to garden terrace
2 Translucent acrylic Opal
panel velcro-fixed to
metal studs with
fluorescent lights behind
3 Skylight with integrated
lighting
4 Upper panel over doors
of spray-painted MDF

5 Pink-sprayed MDF
cupboard doors
6 Pantry door
7 Integrated refrigerator
8 Integrated dishwasher
and microwave
9 Pink-sprayed MDF
external door

**Sections A–A, B–B and C–C
1:50**
1 Translucent acrylic Opal
panel velcro-fixed to
metal studs with
fluorescent lights behind
2 Pantry shelves
3 Fluorescent light behind
translucent acrylic Opal
panel
4 Built-in refrigerator with

pink-sprayed MDF
cupboard doors and
stainless steel handle
5 Pink-sprayed MDF
cupboard doors and
stainless steel handle

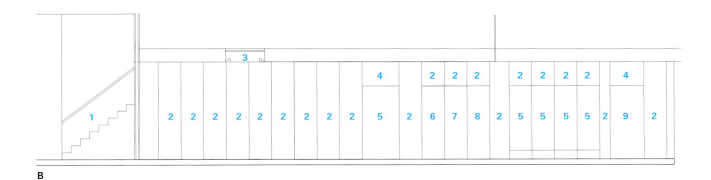

B

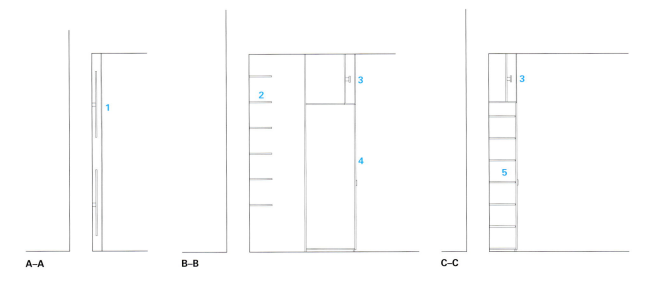

A–A   B–B   C–C

Timber

Turner Castle
Opal House
London, England, UK

Kitchen Elevations C and D
1:50
1 Stainless steel worktop to breakfast bar
2 Touch-catch timber cupboard door
3 Toughened glass balustrade to stair to first floor
4 Solid timber treads
5 Steel stringer

6 Line of pink-painted MDF cupboard doors and translucent acrylic back-lit Opal panels

Right
View of the island bench which is located in front of an expansive wall of clear sheet glass. Behind it, an elegant steel stair with open timber treads and glass balustrade rises to the first floor.

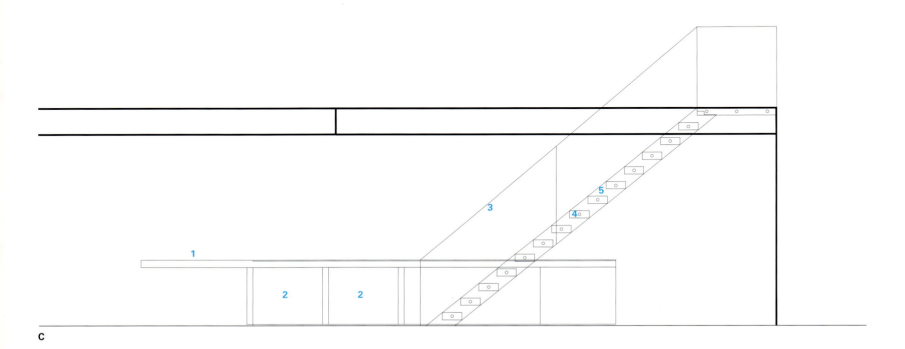

C

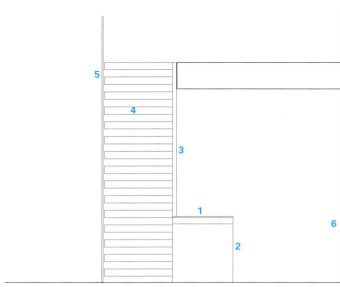

D

Materials
Worktop 6 mm (1/5 inch) thick stainless steel worktop with bespoke integrated sink and drainer by Metal Workshop
Joinery Bespoke Tin Tab burnt oak cupboards and drawers and resin-bonded ply carcassing by Beechway Joinery
Floor Polished concrete screed by Steyson's Granolithic Ltd

Appliances and Fixtures
Taps Vola Mixer Tap
Sink and Drainer Bespoke unit integrated into worktop
Dishwasher Integrated Miele dishwasher

Washing Machine Miele washing machine
Tumble Dryer Miele tumble dryer (in separate utility area)
Refrigerator Integrated Bosch fridge-freezer
Hob and Extractor Miele hob with integrated extractor
Oven Integrated Miele oven
Microwave Integrated Miele microwave
Lighting Ceiling – T5 Fluorescent light fittings in bespoke stainless steel casing with opal acrylic insert by Fagerhult. Wall – T5 Fluorescent light fittings set behind Opal acrylic panels

Project Credits
Completion 2007
Project Architects Cassion Castle, Carl Turner, Lizzie Castle, Susie Hyden, Anna Tenow, Hannah Schneebeli
Structural Engineers Wright Consultancy Group
Main Contractor Turner Castle
Bespoke Furniture Fabrication Turner Castle

CCS Architecture

This renovation of an existing three storey house transforms the interior with a spacious, free-flowing living area that opens up to sweeping views of the city. The house was organized into three distinct areas to accommodate different aspects of the client's life. The ground floor focuses on the entrance and the upgrading of the garage to accommodate the client's collection of vintage cars.

The third floor was transformed into the most private part of the house, including a master bedroom and two guest bedrooms that can be used as children's bedrooms in the future. Between the two is the second floor – a new focal point at the centre of the house for living, cooking and dining. This space utilizes the entire available floor area to let in the maximum amount of daylight and views to the south over San Francisco. Nearly all of the walls were removed and the floor was reorganized as a single continuous space, half of which gathers at a monolithic, minimalist kitchen island.

The client places great importance on cooking and eating with friends and the new second floor responds with generous accommodation for informal entertaining, as well as a stretch of dining area that sits along one long wall of the house. Here, the southern exterior wall has been opened up with a ribbon of windows and a glass door that will access a future deck over the rear garden.

By contrast, the north wall of the floor is lined with an understated but playful grid of shelves for books and artefacts from the client's travels.

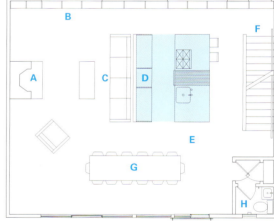

Opposite Left
The kitchen consists of a monolithic stainless steel-topped island bench and a full-height storage wall which incorporates a stainless steel fridge-freezer. The kitchen is open to the adjacent dining area.

Floor Plan
A Fireplace
B Storage shelves
C Living space
D Kitchen storage wall
E Kitchen island
F Stair up from first floor
G Dining area
H WC

Below
The large island bench has space for several stools which help to make the kitchen the social hub of the house. The wall of shelving is built around and over the window, adding a playful and personal touch to the space.

Timber

CCS Architecture
Bernal Heights Residence
San Francisco, California,
USA

Kitchen Plan and Storage Wall Elevation A
1:50
1 Pantry storage
2 Fridge-freezer
3 Stainless steel countertop
4 Gas hob
5 Line of stool recess under
6 Timber chopping board

recessed into countertop
7 Integrated stainless steel sink
8 Painted MDF fixed shelves
9 Painted MDF cupboard door
10 Painted MDF shelves in front of window

Island Bench Elevations B, C, D and E
1:50
1 Double power outlet
2 Sprayed MDF drawer front
3 Gas hob over under-counter oven
4 Timber chopping board recessed into countertop
5 Air vent to dishwasher

below
6 Chrome mixer spout and taps
7 Stainless steel sink
8 Sprayed MDF cupboard door
9 Stainless steel countertop
10 Sprayed MDF end panel
11 Painted MDF kickplate
12 Sprayed MDF cupboard

front
13 Sprayed MDF sliding cupboard front
14 Steel circular section foot rest
15 Painted MDF panel to stool recess

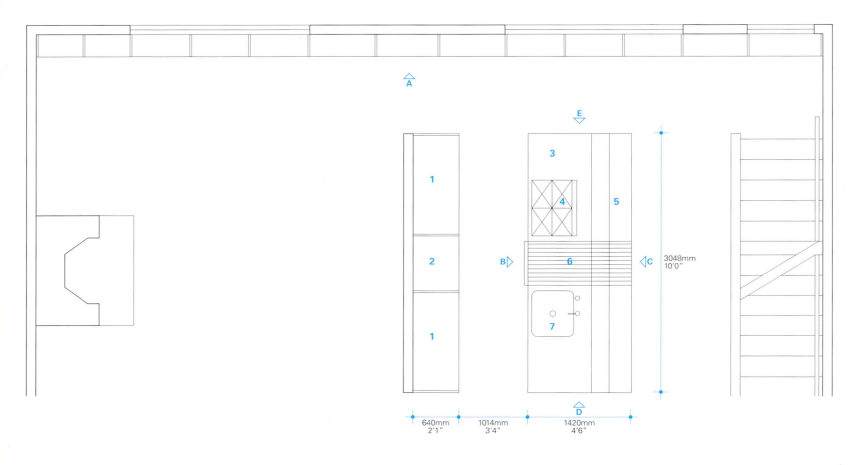

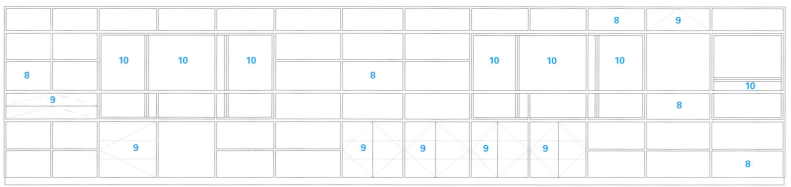

A

Materials
Worktop Stainless steel
Joinery Painted MDF
Floor Walnut

Appliances and Fixtures
Taps Chicago
Spout Chicago
Sink Custom fabricated stainless steel
Disposal Unit Insinkerator
Dishwasher Bosch
Refrigerator Subzero
Oven Dacor
Lighting Recessed low voltage lighting by Capri

Project Credits
Completion 2002
Project Architects Cass Calder Smith, Jordan Geiger
Structural Engineers Kate Simonen
Main Contractor Bay Village Builders

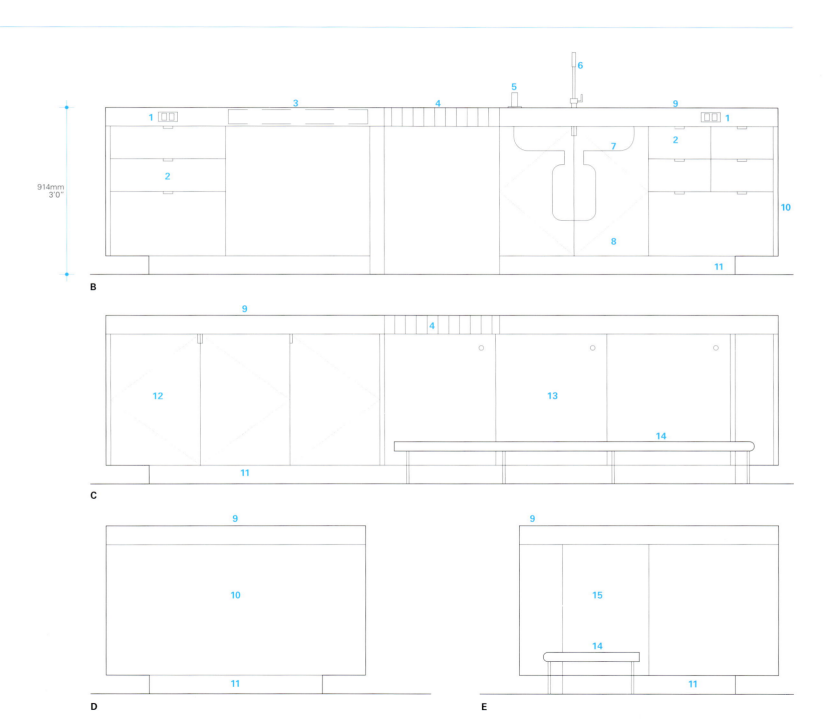

EDH Endoh Design House

Natural Strips II
Tokyo, Japan

This three storey house in the centre of Tokyo was designed for a retired couple. The clients wanted a house that would reflect their new lifestyle while at the same time responding to the inevitably small site in Tokyo.

The ground floor accommodates a small shop with its own dressing room, the first floor is the main living and dining space with kitchen, and the top floor houses the bedroom and bathroom. The structural system makes itself present in the plan – two curved walls of 16 mm (2/3 inch) thick bent plate steel support the concrete floor slabs and enclose the dressing room on the ground floor, create a sculptural feature in the living room and a container for the bathroom upstairs.

The frame is wrapped in a glass curtain wall which, because it is insufficient to insulate the house, is lined with hollow-core clear polycarbonate moveable screens which the inhabitants can close off or open up as they wish according to their needs for privacy and environmental conditions.

A series of galvanized metal, fixed horizontal louvres are attached to the exterior to protect the south and west façades, in particular, from solar gain. The kitchen is located at the north end of the first floor and consists of a compact island bench incorporating a sink and hob, with full-height storage built into the solid north wall behind.

The white doors and panels (constructed from plywood with a white polyester finish) are trimmed in light grey to echo the stainless steel worktop and the strikingly minimal staircase with its single white stringer and aluminium tread nosings.

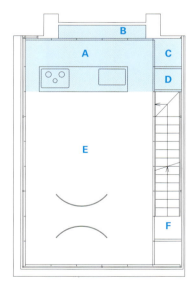

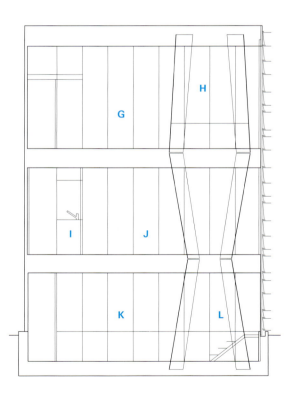

Timber

Masaki Endoh
Natural Strips II
Tokyo, Japan

Kitchen Plan and Elevations A, B and C and Sections A–A and B–B 1:20
1 Line of oven under
2 Gas hob
3 Stainless steel worktop
4 Stainless steel sink
5 Plywood with white polyester finish drawer
6 Plywood with white

polyester finish cupboard front
7 30 mm (1 1/5 inch) diameter drilled hole door pull
8 Chrome spout and mixer tap
9 Line of sink
10 Fixed panel in front of sink
11 Plywood with white

polyester finish sliding cupboard door
12 Plywood with white polyester finish kickplate
13 Microwave oven
14 Oven
15 Power socket
16 Plywood with white polyester finish side panel
17 Utensil drawer

18 Cutlery drawers

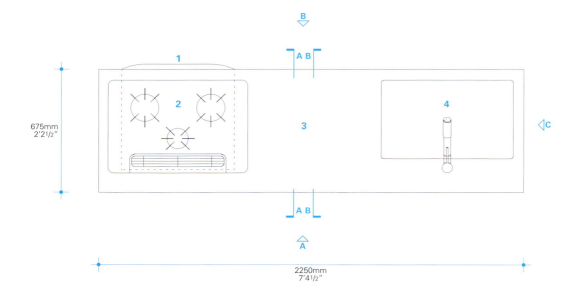

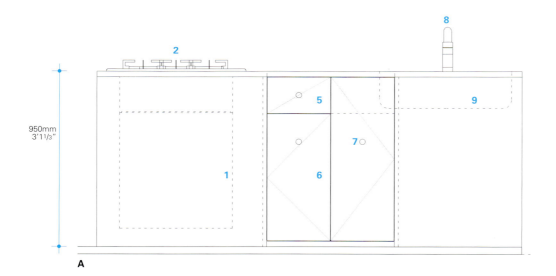

Materials
Worktop Stainless steel
Joinery Plywood with white polyester finish to sliding doors
Floor INAX NPKC-200/PU-21 tiles

Appliances and Fixtures
Taps INAX JF-1450SX(JW) combination tap and spout
including a water purification system
Sink Stainless steel custom made sink
Refrigerator National fridge-freezer
Hob Tokyo Gas HR-P873-DXAAHL(R)
Oven Tokyo Gas SN-860L built-in oven range
Microwave National
Extractor Mitsubishi Electric V-316KSW4 with range hood
exhaust attachment – Mitsubishi Electric P-28MA2
Lighting ENDO ED4458W down lights

Project Credits
Completion 2005
Client Ichiro Chino, Mituko Chino
Project Architects Masaki Endoh, Hiroaki Takada
Structural Engineers Masahiro Ikeda
Main Contractor Sobi Co.Ltd

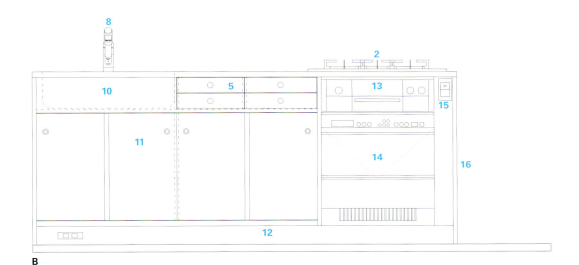

B

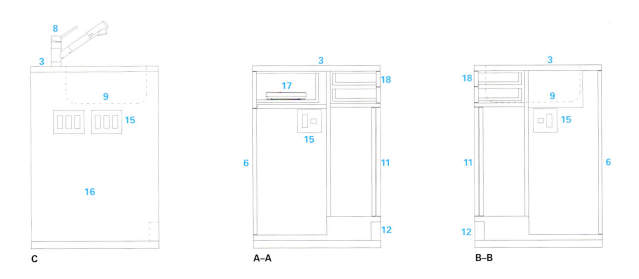

C

A–A

B–B

Donaghy + Dimond Architects

House for Musicians Carrickfin, County Donegal, Ireland

This is a house for music built on a sound at the mouth of an estuary in the Rosses. The site is on a promontory overlooking the confluence of two estuaries at the end of an isthmus, joining what was an island of granite back to the mainland. The footprint of the building straddles a cleft facing south up one estuary and looking east along the Gweedore River to the quartzite cone of Errigal Mountain in the background.

These cardinal points organize the plan around a central kitchen embedded in a hollow in the site, giving glimpses out to the surrounding topography while providing shelter from the elements. A spine of bedrooms lines the house to the north. To the south a sitting room hunkers into the heath by the sea. The kitchen sits between these elements with views of Errigal to the east and the sea to the south. The materials throughout are disposed for acoustic effect and secondary spaces open off the kitchen to create a rich sound for session music while the sitting room is isolated for recording purposes.

A sizeable chimney anchors the house in the landscape and incorporates light shafts and stairs within its girth. The bedrooms are roofed with slates given to the clients as a wedding present, while the lower spaces are turfed over with sod from the site with steps giving access to the sitting room roof from the entrance court.

This roof forms an elevation to the sky, maintains habitat and shelters the space below from the elements. Roof timbers and joinery elements are of larch and the aggregates and sands in the concrete are local, sandblasted outside and polished inside.

Opposite Left
Exterior view of the house showing the stunning beauty of the landscape. The pitched roofed bedroom wing is lit by clerestory windows while the living spaces are anchored to the site by a towering chimney.

Floor Plan
A Master bedroom
B Dressing room
C Terrace
D Kitchen and dining room
E Living room
F Sitting room
G Bedroom
H Bedroom
I Entrance hall
J Entrance
K Cloak room
L Boiler room

Below
The kitchen features Douglas Fir doors to the cabinets that echo the exposed roof structure. Cabinetry is held in place by monolithic cast and polished concrete elements that form both splashback and worktop, as well as carrying on to create a timber-topped bench seat. To the rear of the kitchen, facing the bedrooms, is a gallery storage area incorporated into the rear of the kitchen and seat unit.

Timber

Donaghy + Dimond Architects
House for Musicians
Carrickfin, County Donegal,
Ireland

Kitchen Plan and Elevations
1:20
1 Hearth
2 Step / seat
3 Seat / storage
4 Polished concrete worktop
5 Timber shelf
6 Gas hob
7 Stainless steel sink
8 Sliding door to terrace
9 Dining table
10 Wine storage
11 Drawers to gallery
12 Seat with lift-up panel
13 Integrated refrigerator
14 Integrated oven
15 Dishwasher
16 Drawers
17 Shelving to gallery
18 Polished concrete wall
19 Sliding cabinet door
20 Timber shelf
21 Polished concrete splashback
22 Stainless steel rail
23 Opening to gallery beyond
24 Ledge and back of timber shelf to kitchen
25 Opening to kitchen beyond
26 Polished concrete wall

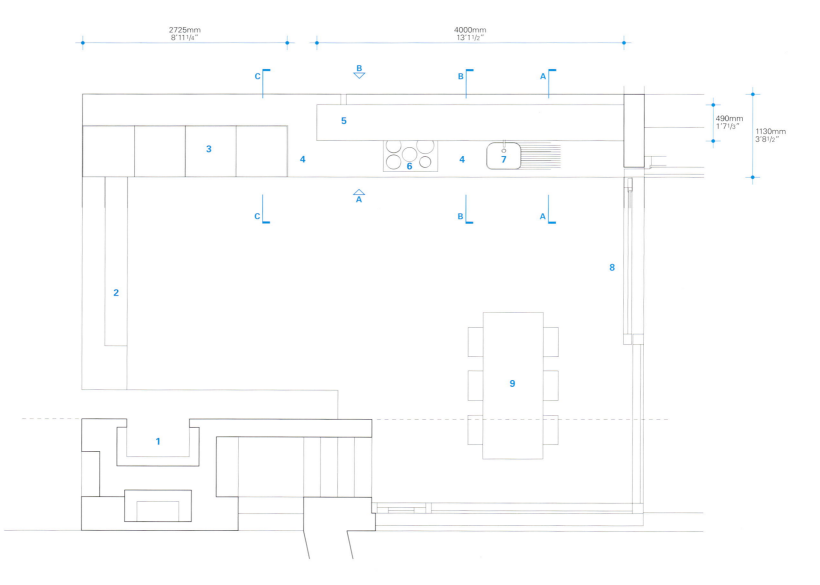

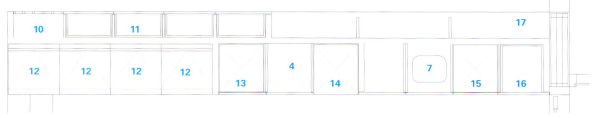

Sectional Plan

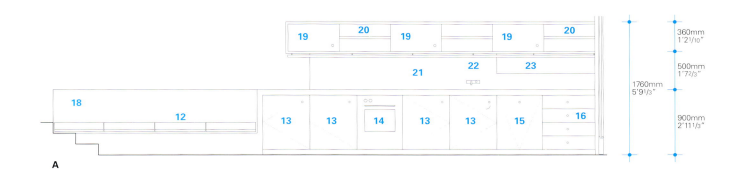

A

360mm
1'2 1/10"

500mm
1'7 2/3"

1760mm
5'9 1/3"

900mm
2'11 1/3"

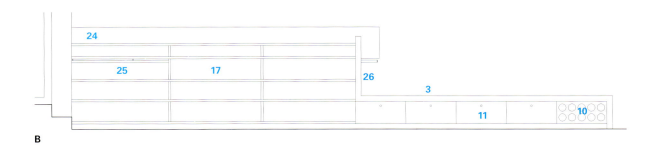

B

Timber

Donaghy + Dimond Architects
House for Musicians
Carrickfin, County Donegal, Ireland

Sections
1:20
1 Ledge with CD storage below
2 Sliding cabinet door
3 Stainless steel rail
4 Timber shelf at opening to gallery
5 Timber shelf
6 Polished concrete worktop
7 Timber shelf
8 Douglas Fir door
9 Recessed timber kickplate
10 Ledge to gallery
11 Shelving to gallery
12 Polished concrete wall
13 Fixed panel to end of shelving
14 Drawers to gallery
15 Seat with lifting panel
16 Timber end panel to shelving unit
17 Bookshelf to end of upper kitchen units
18 Timber end panel to upper kitchen cabinets
19 Line of return to concrete countertop
20 Douglas Fir seat with cushions over
21 Polished concrete plinth

Right
View from the gallery towards the dining area which enjoys views over the estuary. The polished concrete floors and furniture elements contrast with the warmth of the timber joinery.

Far Right
The kitchen includes contrasting storage options, including cupboards, drawers, open shelves and a stainless steel rod for hanging utensils. A cut-out in the concrete splashback allows connection between the kitchen and the gallery behind.

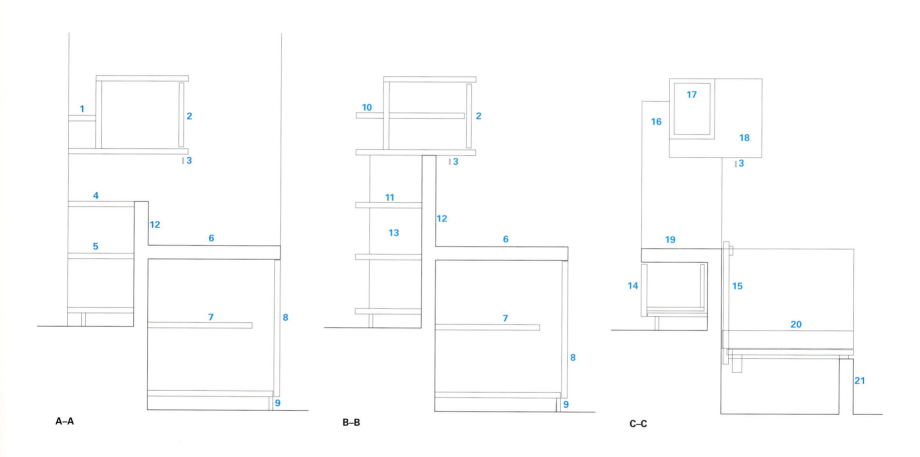

A–A

B–B

C–C

Materials
Worktop Polished concrete using local aggregates
Joinery Douglas Fir
Floor Polished concrete

Appliances and Fixtures
Taps and Spout Vola 132, wall mounted, one handle mixer
Sink Franke 4Rx11033 stainless steel undermounted sink
Dishwasher Smeg maxi-height fully integrated dishwasher
Refrigerator Liebherr, concealed under counter
Hob Smeg, 'classic' stainless steel ultra low profile five burner gas hob
Oven Smeg, 'classic' electric multifunction double under-counter oven
Extractor Automated clerestory window above
Lighting SKK cable light

Project Credits
Completion 2006
Client Mairéad Ní Mhaonaigh and Dermot Byrne
Project Architects Will Dimond, Marcus Donaghy, Steve Larkin
Structural Engineers Downes Associates
Main Contractor Pete Duffy
Joinery Pat Rudkins Joinery

Pablo Fernández Lorenzo and Pablo Redondo Diez

Apartment
Madrid, Spain

This apartment was created for a single person whose minimal needs required only separate spaces for living and sleeping. The tight budget drove the decision to keep the original timber parquet floor, which happily was in good condition, as well as the old radiators, and focus attention on creating a sculptural element that would define the character of the entire space.

It was decided that one large open space for living, dining, cooking, studying and sleeping would be possible in the 55 square metre (592 square feet) space. This was possible given the unusually high 3.7 metre (12 feet) ceilings.

The cleverly designed compact kitchen is the key to the way the living and dining areas

function. Part of the kitchen can be closed off with a glass door, while a sliding glass element covers the counter of the kitchen. With these elements closed, the kitchen is a timber and glass enclosed box in which it is possible to cook without creating noise and smells that might interfere with activities in the living room.

Meanwhile, parts of the kitchen that are useful to access from the dining area are still accessible – a large sink, a dishwasher and cupboard space for plates and glasses. The hand made kitchen, designed and built by the architect, acts as a piece of furniture in the otherwise neutral interior of the apartment, which is emphasized through the use of wax-

finished oak for the cabinetry and countertop.

The outsize sink can be covered with a lid made from the same wood, so that when the lid is closed the worktop is continuous. The part of the kitchen that can be closed is topped by a mezzanine floor, which accommodates the guest bed area with access via a stair constructed from steel cylinders welded to a rectangular pillar that also supports the ceiling. Elsewhere in the apartment, continuity is achieved with a large dining table and desk made from the same wax-finished timber.

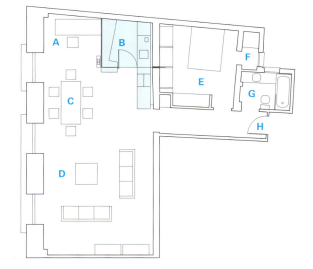

Opposite Left
This impressively compact kitchen is comprised of two main areas. The first is enclosed in a glass box and is topped with a mezzanine sleeping platform, and the second is an open counter area.

Floor Plan
A Study
B Kitchen
C Dining area
D Living area
E Bedroom
F Closet
G Bathroom
H Entrance

Below
A series of vignettes demonstrating the versatility of the covered sink. When closed, the tap can still be used as water drains away through a drilled hole. The panel folds in half and sits back against the wall when fully open.

Bottom
The wax-finished oak used for all of the joinery in the kitchen has been carefully chosen and finished to match the existing parquetry.

Timber

**Pablo Fernández Lorenzo
and Pablo Redondo Diez**
Apartment
Madrid, Spain

**Kitchen Plan and
Elevations A, B and
Sections A–A , B–B
1:50
Sections C–C, D–D , E–E
1:20**

1 Integrated refrigerator
with oak door front
2 Sink
3 Vitroceramic hob and
oven

4 Sink with timber cover
5 Dishwasher
6 Oak work surface
7 Glass pivot door
8 Steel ladder
9 Mezzanine bed platform
10 Stainless steel
splashback
11 Extractor
12 Oak cupboard front
13 Oak drawer fronts

14 Blue lacquered MDF kick
plate
15 Oak panel
16 Glass wall
17 Blue lacquered MDF
cover panel behind sink
18 Sink cover in semi-open
position
19 Sink cover in open
position
20 Desk

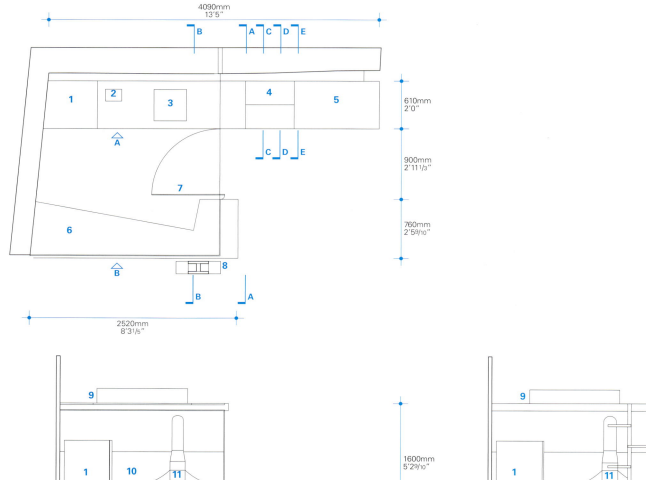

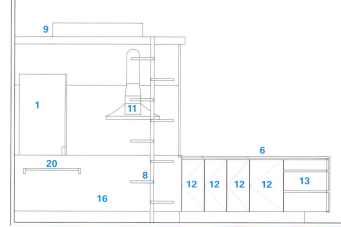

Materials
Worktop Wax-finished oak
Joinery Wax-finished oak
Floor Original oak parqetry
Splashback Stainless steel sheet

Appliances and Fixtures
Taps Ritmonio, diametrotrentacinque
Sink Custom-made stainless steel
Dishwasher Siemens
Refrigerator Siemens integrated fridge-freezer with 16 mm (3/4 inch) thick oak cover panel
Hob Siemens vitroceramic four ring hob
Oven Siemens
Extractor Diáfana, Oscar Tusquets y Lluis Clotet, by BD
Lighting Halogen downlights to ceiling and extractor, lacquered steel Agabekov lights to dining area

Project Credits
Completion 2003
Client Mario Garrido Musso
Project Architects Pablo Fernández Lorenzo, Pablo Redondo Díez
Main Contractor CasaCima S.L

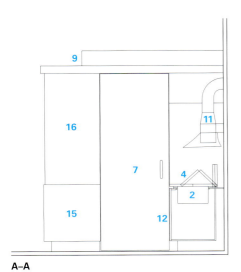

A–A

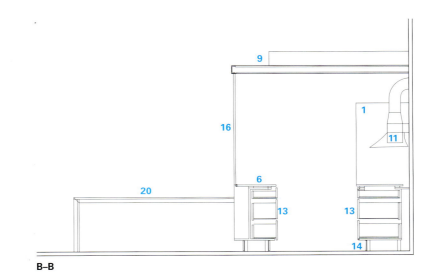

B–B

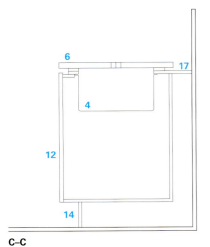

C–C

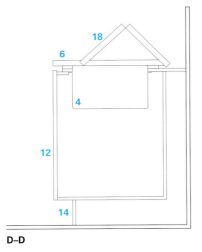

D–D

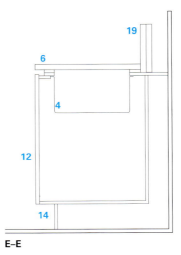

E–E

129

Kaehler Moore
Architects

Milan Guest House
Milan, New York, USA

This house, located in rural upstate New York, takes its cues from the local barn vernacular, which lends itself to the informal residence that was required as a weekend getaway for the clients and their family. The guest house sits at the top of a hill with magnificent views to the west across rolling hills and tree lines to Hunter Mountain.

The house opens to the views and landmarks by way of a glass wall, which reinforces the relationship between the house, its inhabitants and the site. A continuous timber frame structure surrounds the great room that contains the living room, dining area and kitchen. A glass wall running the length of the great room provides a view of the attached deck, pool and landscape. The transparency both connects the great room to the deck and allows for increased natural light, which animates the space as shadows bounce off the walls and floors.

The kitchen, located at the south end of the great room, blends wood and stone elements in keeping with the client's desire to incorporate the distinctive vernacular of local rustic barns. A large piece of dark walnut, found by the architect, was cut and pieced together to form the island countertop, while more dark walnut is found on the sides of the cabinets. Douglas Fir is used for the trusses and horizontal lattice around the kitchen island.

Throughout the great room the floors are made from White Oak with a grey pickled finish. The remaining countertops are black granite with a honed finish. The continuous horizontals found throughout the home are echoed in the horizontal luxor-grey tiles of the backsplash. The timber-frame vaulted ceiling adds height to this elegantly rustic kitchen.

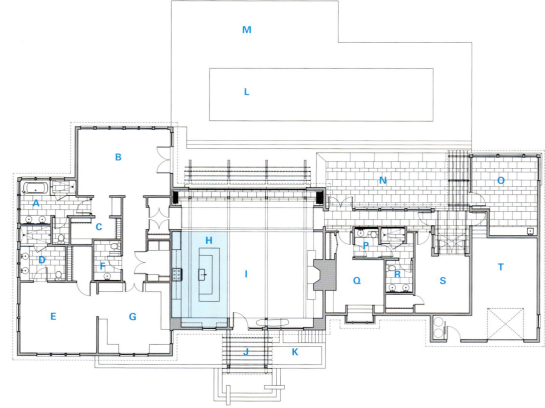

Opposite Left
View of the main terrace with its timber-framed overhang. Double glazed doors to the guest bedroom and double-height glazing to the sun room open up the house to a number of terraces, gardens and views.

Floor Plan
A Master bathroom
B Master bedroom
C Dressing
D Bathroom
E Bedroom
F WC
G Library / study
H Kitchen
I Living room
J Entrance
K Garden
L Swimming pool
M Terrace
N Garden terrace
O Sun room
P Guest bathroom
Q Guest bedroom 1
R Guest WC
S Guest bedroom 2
T Garage

Below
The main feature of the kitchen is the generously-scaled island bench with its cantilevered top of walnut which provides seating space for family and guests to gather at the kitchen, which is itself at the centre of the house.

131

Timber

Kaehler Moore Architects
Milan Guest House
Milan, New York, USA

Kitchen Plan, Elevations A and B, and Sections A–A and B–B
1:50

1 Integrated fridge-freezer
2 Line of upper cabinets
3 Oven
4 Honed black granite worktop
5 Pantry
6 Honed black granite

raised worktop to island
7 Stainless steel sink
8 Raised island worktop in walnut
9 Upper cabinet with adjustable shelves
10 Walnut end panel
11 Under-cabinet walnut trim with concealed lights
12 Food prep area with

honed black granite honed worktop
13 Adjustable shelves
14 Perimeter walnut trim
15 Custom painted pantry door
16 Custom painted cabinet door with adjustable shelves
17 Custom painted oven hood cover

18 Luxor grey tile splashback
19 Custom painted drawer
20 Custom painted panel to freezer
21 Custom painted panel to refrigerator
22 Douglas Fir lattice around base of island
23 Tap and spout with hand spray

24 Wine chiller
25 Custom painted base cabinet
26 Custom painted sink cabinet
27 Dishwasher
28 Framing and structure for Douglas Fir lattice

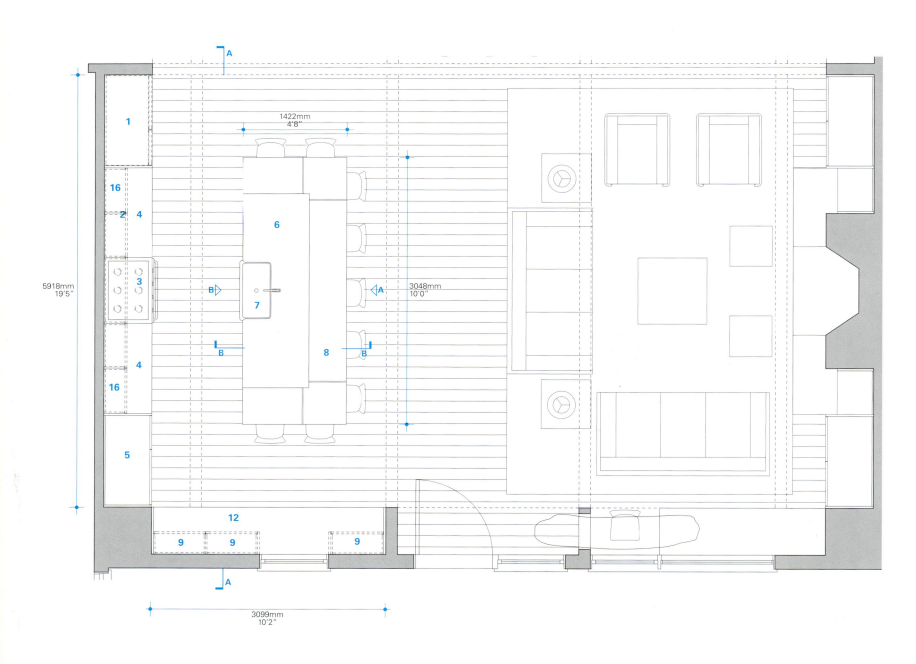

Materials

Worktop 30 mm (1¹/5 inch) thick black granite honed and sealed, island raised surface to island 30 mm (1¹/5 inch) thick walnut
Joinery Custom cabinets
Floor 101 mm (4 inch) wide character grade White Oak with grey pickled finish and three coats of water-based polyurethane
Tiles Luxor grey 44 x 450 mm (1³/4 x 17³/4 inch) tiles with sealer

Appliances and Fixtures

Taps Kohler 'Vinnata' kitchen tap with hand spray
Sink Kohler 'Verity Apron Front' under counter kitchen sink
Dishwasher ASKO dishwasher with stainless steel front
Refrigerator Subzero 632/S side by side Refrigerator
Wine Chiller Subzero 424 wine storage
Oven Viking Professional Series VDSC
Microwave Sharp Insight Microwave Drawer KB-601 5KS
Extractor Broan-Nu Tone 'Rangemaster Power Pack'
Lighting WAK track lighting with halogen fixtures and Hera under-cabinet recessed halogen spotlights

Project Credits

Completion 2006
Project Architects Laura Kaehler, Mathew Arnott, Gregory McGuire
Structural Engineers Edward Stanley Engineers
Main Contractor Pompa Construction

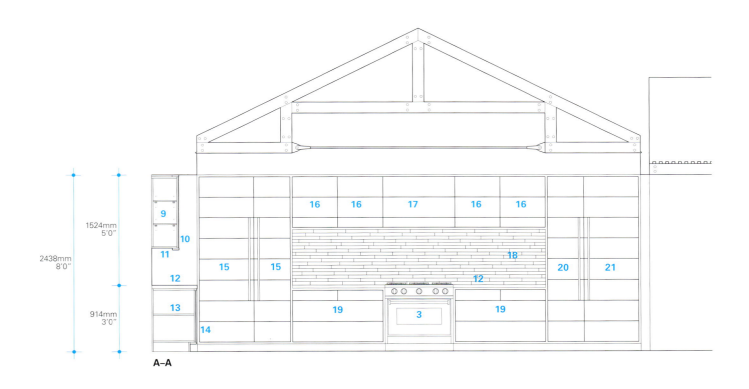

A–A

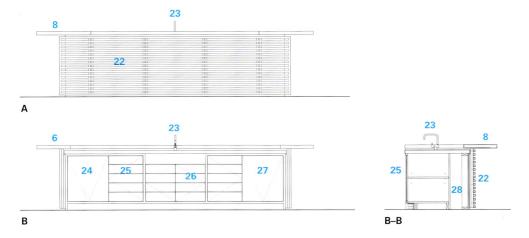

A

B

B–B

Westarchitecture

This kitchen is part of a highly tailored refurbishment and reconfiguration of a mews house in Notting Hill, London. In common with many mews houses, the bedrooms are on the ground floor with the living areas positioned on the upper floors to take advantage of the light.

A bespoke kitchen replaces one which was previously positioned in the extension off the main living space. The owner had noticed that when he had friends over for dinner, in order to converse with him they congregated around the kitchen rather than relaxing in the living space. It was therefore important that the new kitchen had a much more direct relationship with the living space and that the owner could easily communicate with guests while he prepared dinner.

The main kitchen fills the entire side wall of the living space along with a bank of storage. The extent of the kitchen is defined by a 50 millimetre (2 inch) margin detail which unifies it whilst visually separating it from the storage above. The language and detailing of the kitchen continues into the dining area to visually connect it and to emphasize the horizontality and linearity of the kitchen.

The island unit sits at the top of the staircase forming a balustrade to two sides of the opening whilst also supporting a cantilevered glass balustrade. This enabled the floor to be cut back over the stair at a much sharper angle, therefore gaining some extra floor space.

The side of the island unit that faces the living area accommodates a music and media hub. Dark oak veneer with a graphite stain was chosen for the kitchen to complement the lighter timber of the floor and the worktops which are all Sterling Grey Zodiaq Quartz. Internal linings are pistachio green – like a Paul Smith suit, the serious exterior belies a colourful lining which is seldom seen by anyone but the owner.

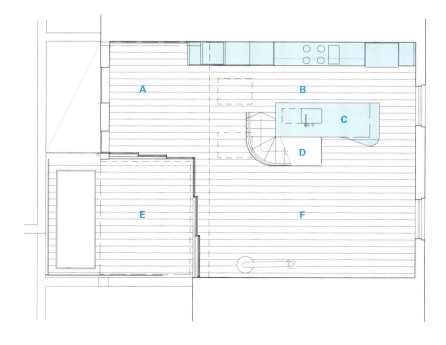

Opposite Left
Originally arranged as stabling with living quarters above, Victorian mews houses, of which this is a typical example, have become popular as small inner-city dwellings.

Floor Plan
A Dining area
B Kitchen
C Island bench
D Stair to lower level
E Terrace
F Living area

Below
A cantilevered glass balustrade curves around the stair which wraps around two sides of the island bench. Above the storage wall, additional storage is concealed by white-painted cupboard doors.

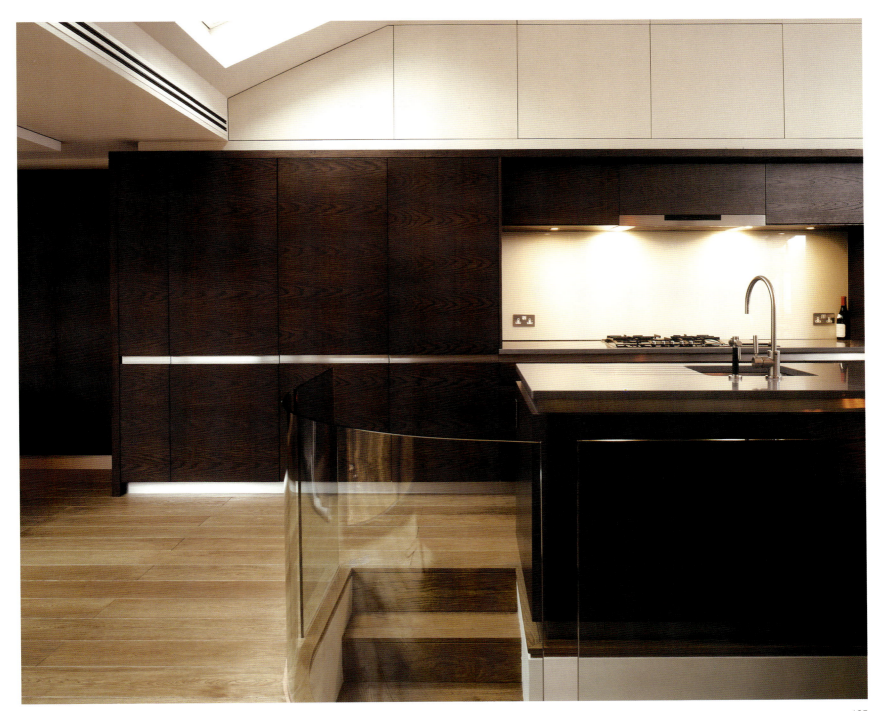

Westarchitecture
Pembridge House
London, England, UK

**Kitchen Plan, Sections
A–A, Section B–B and
Elevations A and B
1:50**

1 Oak veneer storage
  cupboards
2 Washing machine and
  tumble dryer
3 Zodiaq Quartz worktop
4 Gas hob
5 Gas BBQ

6 Refrigerator
7 Pull-out larder
8 Dotted line of skylight
  above
9 Line of draining grooves
  in worktop
10 Stainless steel sink
11 Worktop prep area
12 Breakfast bar
13 Tumble dryer
14 Washing machine

15 Extractor hood
16 Oak veneer drawer fronts
17 Oven
18 Oak veneer cupboard
  front
19 Chrome mixer tap
20 Oak veneer fixed panel
21 Cupboard for media
  equipment
22 Dishwasher
23 Pull-out bins and

recycling storage
24 White-painted high level
  storage cupboards

A–A

Materials
Worktop Zodiaq Quartz in Sterling Grey
Joinery Oak veneer with graphite stain
Floor Engineered Oak
Splash back Low iron glass back painted as wall colour

Appliances and Fixtures
Taps Dornbracht
Spout Dornbracht
Sink Franke
Dishwasher Siemens
Refrigerator Maytag
Hob Siemens
Oven Siemens
Microwave Siemens
Extractor Siemens
Lighting Iguzzini Zoom low voltage spots

Project Credits
Completion 2007
Client Erik van der Aggigard
Project Architects Graham West
Structural Engineers Webb Yates Engineers
Main Contractor A Price Ltd

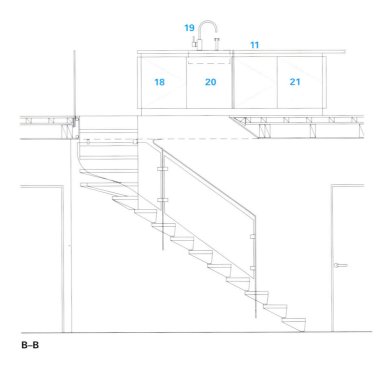

B–B

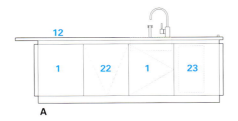

A

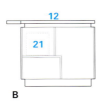

B

Morgan Cronin

Cronin Beach House
Tairua, Coromandel, New Zealand

The owner of this house, located on the east coast of the Coromandel Peninsula on the north island of New Zealand, required a kitchen for entertaining friends and family in a relaxed atmosphere to suit their modern beach house.

The kitchen, consisting of two island benches and a storage wall, is placed within a large rectangular room that has stunning views in both directions. The two island benches, constructed with white Corian worktops and American White Ash veneer for the joinery, provide a division between the living and dining areas, enabling the cook to interact with guests, either in the lounge, at the dining table or even outside.

The worktops incorporate an integrated Corian sink and drainage area within the 12 millimetre (1/2 inch) thick worktop to achieve a slim profile to the edge. The island cabinetry, positioned to line up with the full-height pantry and storage wall, appears to float, enabling the solid American Ash timber floor to continue throughout the room, enhancing the feeling of space. Plumbing and electrical services were positioned early on in the construction process ensuring these services could be concealed within the Corian end panels.

The pantry wall, which includes a large fully concealed integrated refrigerator, has an aluminium kickplate and recessed handle rail that line up with the two islands. Both pantry and crockery cabinets include bench space with shelves above and the pantry conceals the kitchen's second sink, which provides extra space for food preparation and concealing dirty dishes whilst entertaining. It also serves as a café bar with built-in coffee machine and microwave.

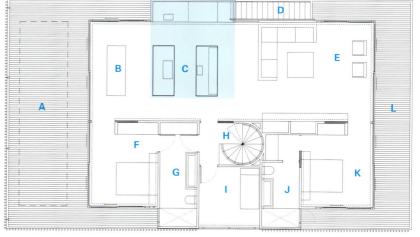

Opposite Left
The beach house features a timber brise-soleil to three façades which both lends privacy to the terraces and provides shade.

Left
View of the kitchen and living room. A custom designed ulta-slim stainless steel extractor unit floats above the induction hob.

Floor Plan
A Terrace
B Dining area
C Kitchen
D External stair
E Living room
F Bedroom
G Bathroom
H Stair to first floor
 I Bedroom
J Bathroom
K Bedroom
L Terrace

Below Left
All of the door and drawer fronts are finished in American White Ash veneer with simple aluminium linear finger pulls. The two island units are complemented by a wall of full-height cupboards which conceal an integrated fridge-freezer, pantry and additional preparation space. Flush door and drawer pulls echo the shadow line of the island benches.

Timber

Morgan Cronin
Cronin Beach House
Tairua, Coromandel,
New Zealand

**Kitchen Plan,
Elevations A, B, C and D
and Section A–A
1:50**
1 Integrated fridge-freezer
2 Crockery cupboard
3 Pantry sink
4 American Ash veneer to
cupboard fronts
5 Stool recess under island
bench
6 Drainage panel in Corian
worktop
7 Corian sink
8 Corian worktop
9 Corian end panel
10 Drawers under
11 Induction hob with
double oven under
12 American Ash veneer to
drawer fronts
13 Stainless steel
suspended extractor
14 Oven
15 Shelves to pantry
cupboard
16 Microwave and coffee
maker
17 Pantry cupboard with
open shelving
18 Microwave
19 Coffee maker
20 Integrated dishwasher

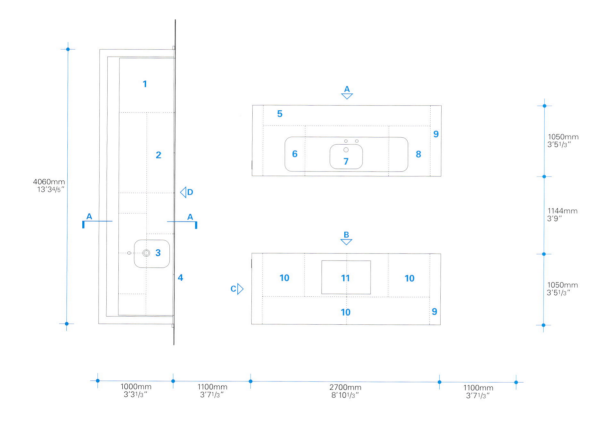

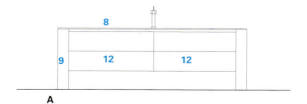

Materials
Worktop Corian Cameo White by Benchworks
Joinery American White Ash veneer from Gibsons with
Triptrap white oil finish from Design Denmark
Hardware Blum hinges and Blum stainless steel Tandembox
drawers all from Sanco
Floor American White Ash from BBS Timber finished in
TripTrap white oil from Design Denmark

Appliances and Fixtures
Taps and Spout MGS Boma from InResidence
Sink Custom made bowls in Corian Cameo White
Dishwasher Miele fully integrated dishwasher
Refrigerator Integrated Fisher & Paykel 440TRE
Hob Miele induction hob
Oven Miele
Microwave Miele combination microwave
Extractor Crosbie Stainless Steel custom made extractor
Coffee Machine Miele
Lighting Lumen Design

Project Credits
Completion 2005
Client Morgan Cronin
Project Architects Morgan Cronin, Scott Fowler
Structural Engineers Lake Engineering Consultants Ltd
Lighting Consultant Lumen Lighting Design

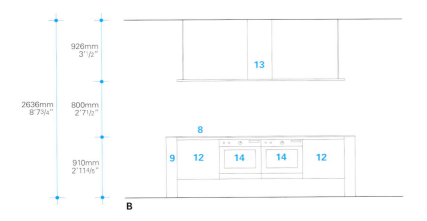

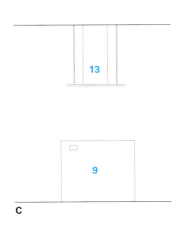

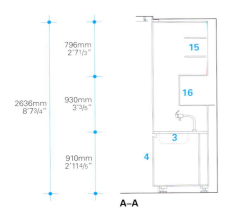

Steel Kitchens

Tzannes Associates

Parsley Bay Residence Sydney, New South Wales, Australia

Located on Sydney's spectacular harbour front, the design for the Parsley Bay residence evolved through an intensive collaboration between the architects and the client. The kitchen forms the anchor for the informal family living and dining areas which open directly onto the spectacular waterfront views.

The centre of kitchen activity is focussed around a 3.3 metre (11½ feet) long Bedonia stone worktop formed from a single slab. This is supported on stainless steel-clad joinery and Bedonia stone 'blades' and cantilevered at one corner to allow for casual eating and socializing on bar stools.

The primary kitchen work areas are formed around a 5.5 metre (18 feet) long frameless glass window which opens to a wall of bougainvillea. The kitchen surfaces are constructed from fully clad stainless steel joinery with seamless integrated sinks. A prep kitchen area including additional wash-up areas, appliance cupboards and a small kitchen office and work area is a continuation of the primary kitchen but can be closed off by means of a large sliding door panel.

Located between and adjacent to the main kitchen and the prep kitchen is a walk-in pantry with commercial ice maker, fridge and freezer to cater for larger gatherings. The stainless steel elements are taken through into the pantry in the form of stainless steel edge strips to the shelving. An external BBQ area is a continuation of the primary kitchen opening via fully retracting glass doors and using the same palette of materials.

The approach to detailing was to provide a seamless integral aesthetic, for example the benchtop edge detailing evolved to match the selected range cooker. Door and drawer pulls were integrated into the panel edges and the resultant recessed shadow lines used to articulate the overall composition.

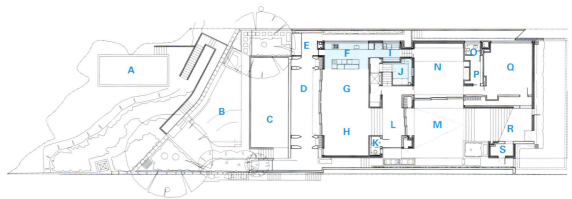

Left
The main kitchen is comprised of an island bench overlooking the dining area, and a wall of workspace with overhead cupboards with a clear-glazed window acting as a splashback looking over a bougainvillea garden. The BBQ terrace (centre) is accessed directly from the kitchen.

Below Left
View of the main kitchen which leads to a prep kitchen housing the large appliances beyond. All surfaces, including worktops, drawers and cupboard fronts are clad in stainless steel.

Below Right
View of the prep kitchen which leads into the living room via a short flight of stairs. The stainless steel is continued in the end wall panels and book shelves.

Steel

Tzannes Associates
Parsley Bay Residence
Sydney, New South Wales,
Australia

**Kitchen Plan
1:50**
1 Stainless steel
   countertop
2 Gas hob
3 Line of overhead
   cupboards
4 Clear glazed window
5 Stainless steel sink
6 Coffee machine
7 Storage cupboard

8 Stainless steel fridge-
   freezer
9 Stainless steel sink with
   insinkerator
10 Dishwasher under
11 Oven under
12 Undermounted stainless
   steel sink
13 Cupboard under
14 Drawers under
15 Refrigerator under

16 Microwave under
17 Badonia stone worktop
18 Void under for stools
19 Stainless steel worktop
   with shelves over
20 Filing drawers under
21 Ice machine
22 Pantry shelving with
   stainless steel edge strip
23 Access panel over
24 Glass-fronted fridge

25 Freezer
26 Stair to living room

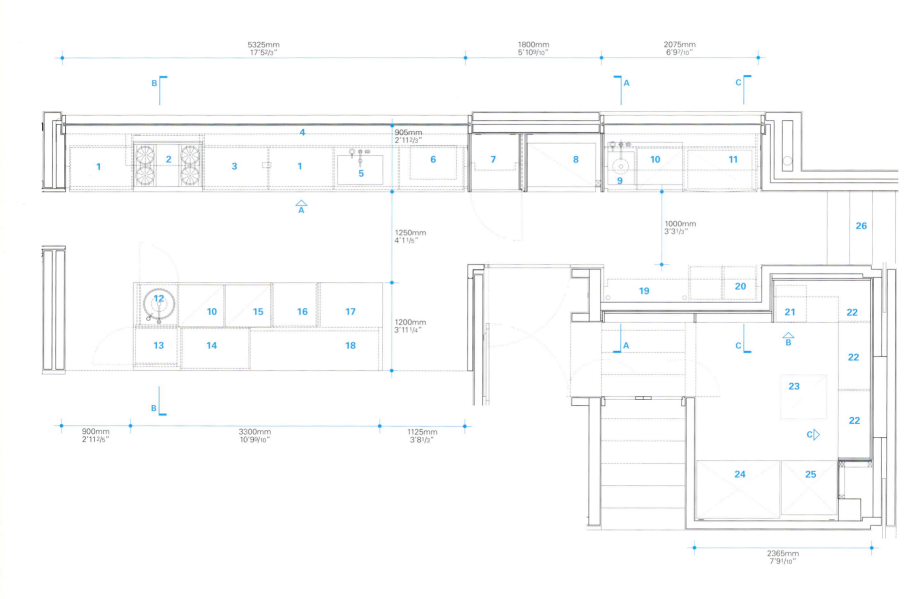

Elevation A, and Section A–A and B–B

1:50

1 Stainless steel cupboard front with adjustable shelves behind
2 Range hood behind
3 Stainless steel drawers
4 Free-standing oven
5 Stainless steel worktop
6 Window behind
7 Hot and cold zip tap
8 Stainless steel sink behind fixed stainless steel panel
9 Hydro zip unit behind
10 Coffee machine
11 Stainless steel cupboard front
12 Stainless steel
refrigerator
13 Stainless steel freezer
14 Chrome mixer tap and spout
15 Insinkerator unit
16 Integrated dishwasher
17 Oven
18 Under-stair area
19 Under-stair shelving with profiled plasterboard
ceiling
20 Stainless steel shelves
21 Open to kitchen beyond
22 Concealed lighting
23 Services zone
24 Stainless steel cupboard front with removable access panel to range hood behind
25 Stainless steel sink
26 Bedonia stone worktop to island bench
27 Bedonia stone front panel to island bench
28 Gas hob

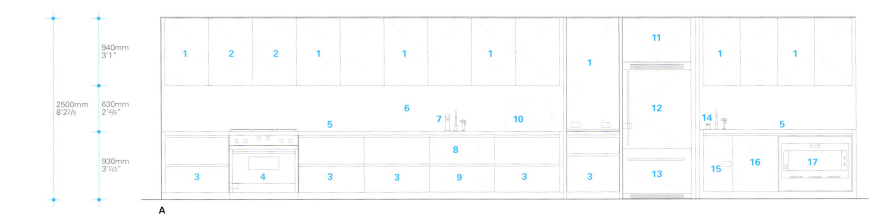

A

A–A

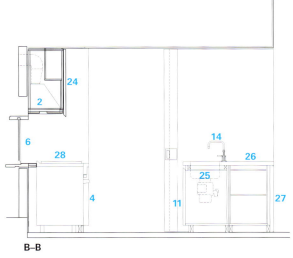

B–B

Tzannes Associates
Parsley Bay Residence
Sydney, New South Wales,
Australia

**Section C–C and
Elevations B and C
1:50**

1 Stainless steel cupboard
with adjustable shelf
2 Concealed lighting
3 Window
4 Stainless steel worktop
5 Services zone
6 Oven
7 Stainless steel open
shelving
8 Stainless steel filing
drawers
9 Painted timber fixed
pantry shelves with
stainless steel edge strip
10 Painted timber adjustable
pantry shelves with
stainless steel edge strip
11 Glass-fronted fridge
12 Stainless steel door to
kitchen
13 Ice machine
14 Hinged access panel in
ceiling
15 Freezer

Opposite Left
View of the prep kitchen
looking towards the main
kitchen.

Opposite Right
The pantry allows easy
access to food and
equipment stored on open
shelves.

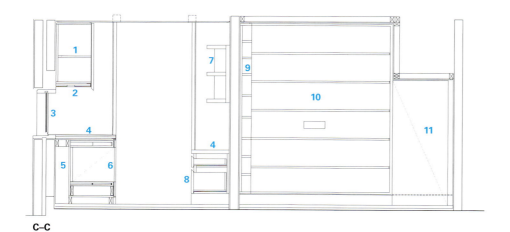

C–C

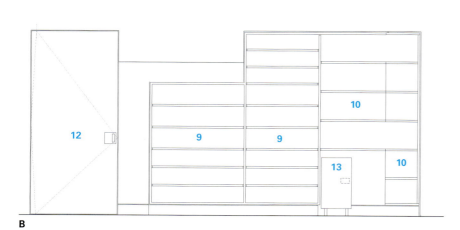

B

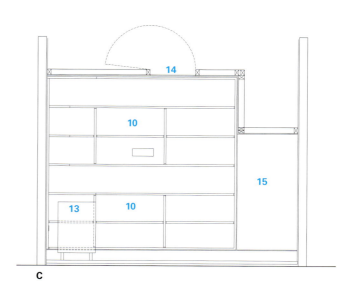

C

Materials
Worktop Bedonia stone worktop to island, stainless steel to wall worktop
Joinery Stainless steel clad drawer and cupboard fronts and shelving
Floor Sandblasted Isernia limestone

Appliances and Fixtures
Taps and Spout Dornbracht 'Meta O2' single lever mixer
Sink Island – Franke undermounted sink. Benchtop – integrated stainless steel sink
Disposal Unit In-Sink-Erator model 75
Dishwasher Miele with integrated stainless steel panel
Refrigerator (1) Jenn-Air full-height refrigerator
(2) Liebherr under-bench fridge. (3) Skope fridge and freezer
Oven Main oven – Viking. Prep kitchen – Gaggenau
Microwave Panasonic with trim kit, model NN-T7046S
Extractor Qasar rangehood with mild stainless steel casing

Project Credits
Completion 2006
Project Architects Alec Tzannes, Phillip Rossington, Bruce Chadlowe, Nadia Zhao, Emma Webster
Structural Engineers Sinclair Knight Merz
Hydraulic Consultant Whipps Wood Consulting
Landscape Consultant Sue Barnsley Design
Main Contractor Infinity Constructions
Lighting Consultant Light 2
Electrical Consultant Haron Robson

Welsh + Major Architects

Albert Street Residence
Sydney, NSW, Australia

This house is located in a quiet, elevated street, one of an unusual row of single storey terraces that turn their backs to the street. The original front entrances to the row face onto a communal cliff-top garden that is no longer accessible from the street. The creation of a new street presence and the definition of a new entry sequence is a fundamental component of the renovation.

The new work is a sequence of external and internal spaces that play with the concepts of solidity and transparency. The entrance opens onto a private courtyard through which one passes to reach the new extension. This is expressed as a distinct pavilion, allowing the continuity of the old terrace row beyond to remain intact. This modern living pavilion, containing living, dining and kitchen areas, is the hub of the house and opens onto the entry courtyard which also serves as an extension of the living space.

Located through necessity on the southern side of the house, the pavilion extends towards the boundary to capture northern light along the side of the house. A high-level concrete beam defines the space, provides eaves protection and creates an alcove for much needed storage. A clerestory on three sides of the pavilion separates the concrete beam from a 'floating' ceiling, capturing natural light. The overhanging deciduous trees provide protection and a cool green aspect in summer which also allows a profusion of light to enter in winter.

The concrete beam also defines the open kitchen. A stainless steel cooking alcove is inserted into the wall of kitchen joinery in a controlled expression of this functional space.

Opposite Left
The kitchen – comprised of a full-height storage wall into which a cooking recess sits, and an island bench – is adjacent to a corner window fitted with glazing that stacks away to open the space up to a small side courtyard.

Floor Plan
A Communal garden
B Verandah
C Bedroom 1
D Bedroom 2
E Study
F Courtyard
G Bathroom
H Kitchen
I Dining area
J Living area
K Courtyard garden
L Street entrance

Below Left
View from the street where an L-shaped concrete portal announces the entrance. Steel-framed timber panels and a steel gate complete the composition.

Bottom Left
Aerial view showing the full width openable glazing to the living room with the clerestory windows above that wrap around three sides of the living spaces below.

Below Right
Facing directly onto the living spaces, the detailing of the kitchen is expressed as a minimal composition. All white joinery matches painted white walls, while accents of stainless steel are reserved for the cooking recess and countertop.

Steel

Welsh + Major Architects
Albert Street Residence
Sydney, NSW, Australia

**Kitchen Plan and
Elevation A
1:20**

1 Bathroom
2 Two-pack polyurethane paint finished storage cupboards
3 Stainless steel countertop to cooking recess
4 Gas hob
5 Integrated fridge-freezer
6 Line of raised ceiling over
7 Stainless steel sink
8 Stainless steel countertop
9 Drawers behind white laminate cupboard fronts
10 Extractor unit behind two-pack polyurethane paint finished panels
11 Stainless steel

splashback to cooking recess
12 Electrical outlet
13 Oven
14 Integrated freezer
15 Integrated refrigerator
16 Kickplate with aluminium grille
17 Opening to hallway beyond

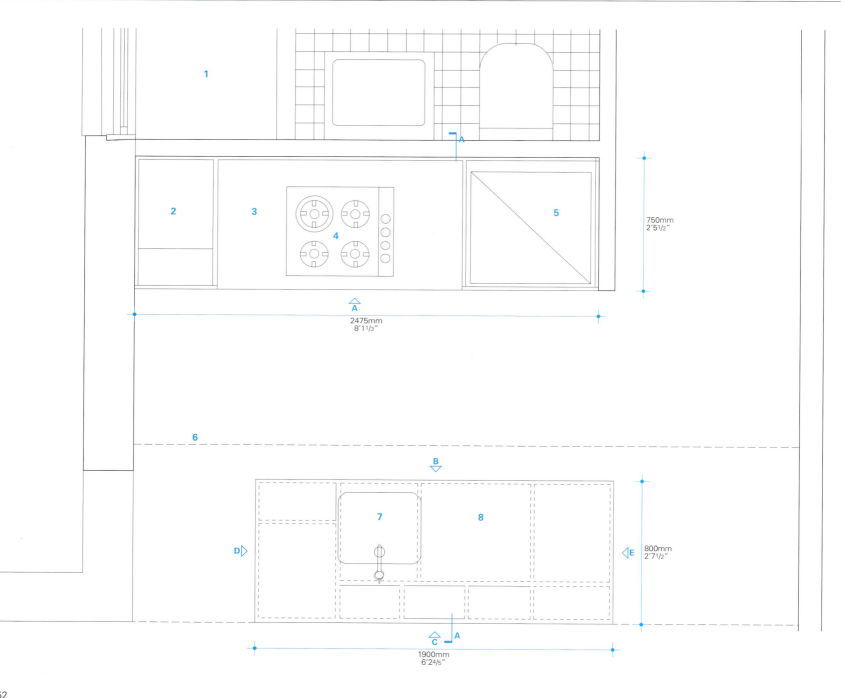

750mm
2'5 1/2"

A
2475mm
8'1 1/3"

B

D

E
800mm
2'7 1/2"

C
A
1900mm
6'2 4/5"

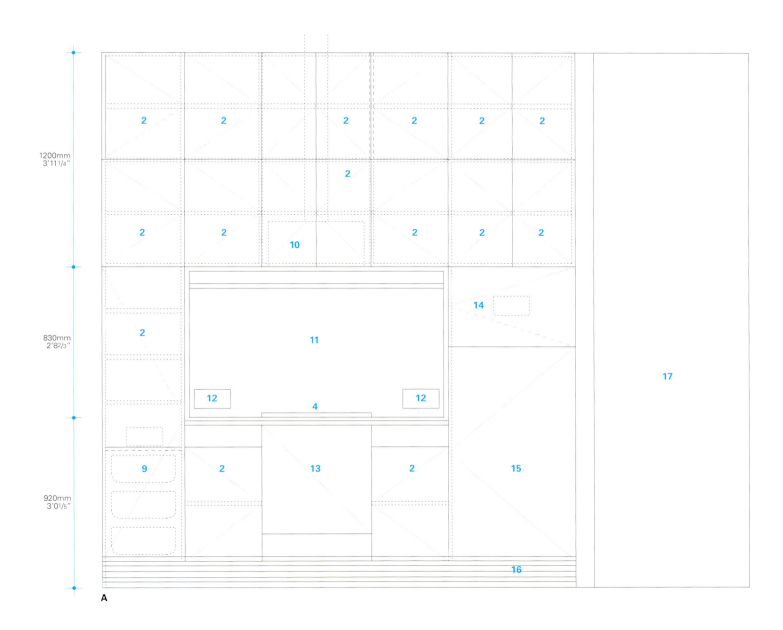

1200mm
3'11¹/₄"

830mm
2'8²/₃"

920mm
3'0¹/₅"

A

Steel

Welsh + Major Architects
Albert Street Residence
Sydney, NSW, Australia

Section A–A
1:20
1 Suspended task
   lighting
2 Glazed window beyond
3 Stainless steel tap
4 MDF carcass with white
   laminate cupboard fronts
5 Solid kickplate
6 Stainless steel
   splashback

to cooking recess
7 Gas hob
8 Timber stud wall
9 Kickplate with aluminium
   grille

Island Unit
Elevations B, C, D and E
1:20
1 Stainless steel
   countertop

2 MDF carcass with white
   laminate cupboard fronts
3 Dishwasher
4 Stainless steel tap
5 Stainless steel sink
6 Sink waste
7 MDF carcass with white
   laminate drawer fronts
8 Solid kickplate
9 Two-pack polyurethane
   paint finished shelf

10 Two-pack polyurethane
   paint finished bottle
   storage
11 Two-pack polyurethane
   paint finished side panel

A–A

154

Materials
Worktop Stainless steel
Joinery Two pack polyurethane on high moisture resistant (HMR) MDF substrate
Floor 150 x 19 mm (6 x 3/4 inch) Grey Ironbark strip flooring

Appliances and Fixtures
Spout Roger Seller Nostromo
Sink Stainless steel sink, fully integrated into island bench
Dishwasher Miele fully integrated dishwasher
Refrigerator Fisher and Paykel fully integrated fridge-freezer
Hob Miele gas hob
Oven Miele
Microwave Sharp
Extractor Smeg
Lighting Louis Poulsen 'Reduced' over benchtop and Targetti Squadra uplighting

Project Credits
Completion 2003
Client Chris Major and David Welsh
Project Architects Chris Major, David Welsh
Structural Engineers Simpson Design Associates
Quantity Surveyor Milliken Berson Madden

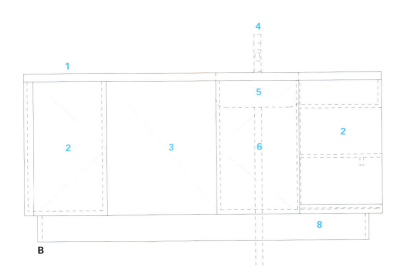

B

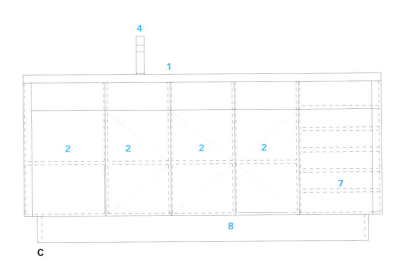

C

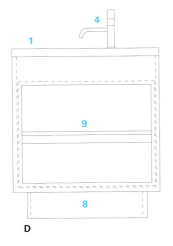

D

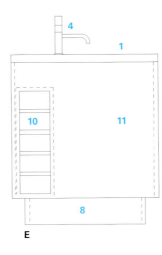

E

155

Tezuka Architects + Masahiro Ikeda

Engawa House
Tokyo, Japan

The Engawa House was designed to accommodate an extended family. To the north of the main site is the grandparents' home, with the eldest son and his family living on the second floor, while the daughter and her husband decided to settle when a property to the south of the main site went on sale. Next door is the main building, where the eldest son and his wife manage a construction company.

The building-to-land ratio in the area is typically high, often resulting in houses that take up the entire plot leaving no room for outdoor space. Here, however, a long narrow building borders the road with an open area along the northern side to provide space for an inner garden. The wall facing the road rises to a height of 2.2 metres (7 feet), with clerestory windows that protect the family's privacy while opening up views of the sky. On the other side, floor-to-ceiling sliding glass doors provide full access to the garden. The result is an expansive but private courtyard space encased between two L-shaped buildings.

The nine glass doors are framed in timber to create a monolithic sense of the structure. Pale timber continues in the interior where the floor, cupboards, shelving and furniture create a unified, calm open living space for the entire family. The kitchen – essentially a large stainless steel island unit – stands between a run of full-height timber cupboards and the dining table at the centre of the house.

On one side of the island, the joinery rises up to create both a visual shield to the dining area and a place to put cooking materials. On the other side are accommodated all of the appliances including gas hob, oven and dishwasher.

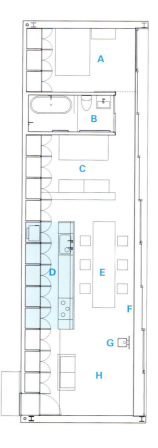

Opposite Left
The house takes its name – *Engawa* – from the attenuated garden that is shared by both houses that face onto it. In traditional Japanese architecture, an *engawa* is a verandah or semi-enclosed social space.

Floor Plan
A Master bedroom
B Bathroom
C Bedroom
D Kitchen
E Dining area
F Full-height glass doors
G Wood burning stove
H Living area

Left
The stainless steel kitchen island stands at the centre of the house. To the right, bedrooms and bathrooms are defined by two metre (6.5 feet) high partitions, leaving the upper space free of divisions.

Below Left
The entire length of the house, from the bedrooms at one end to the living area at the other, open up to the courtyard garden via sliding glass doors, enabling all of the extended family to meet and socialize in the garden or in the kitchen and dining area.

Steel

**Tezuka Architects +
Masahiro Ikeda**
Engawa House
Tokyo, Japan

**Kitchen Island Plan and
Elevation,
Cross section
1:50**

1 Stainless steel
   countertop
2 Integrated stainless steel
   sink
3 Elevated countertop with
   concealed fluorescent
   lighting

4 Gas hob
5 Stainless steel legs
6 Stainless steel
   splashback
7 Void / storage
8 Dishwasher
9 Stainless steel sink
10 Fixed panel below sink
11 Integrated freezer
   with stainless steel
   cupboard fronts

12 Integrated refrigerator
   with stainless steel
   cupboard fronts
13 Stainless steel cupboard
   front
14 Oven
15 Clear glazed clerestory
   windows
16 Full-height timber pantry
   cupboards
17 Painted partition wall

beyond
18 Stainless steel island
   bench
19 Timber floor
20 Sliding glass doors
21 Wood burning stove
22 Courtyard garden
23 Under-floor air-
   conditioning unit

Right
View of the kitchen from the
living area. Full-height timber
cupboards behind the
stainless steel island bench
provide general storage as
well as accommodating an
integrated refrigerator.

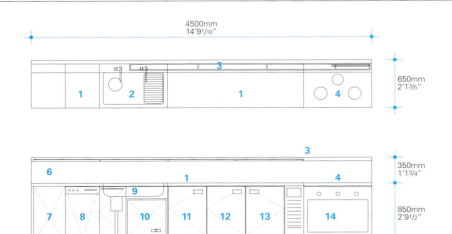

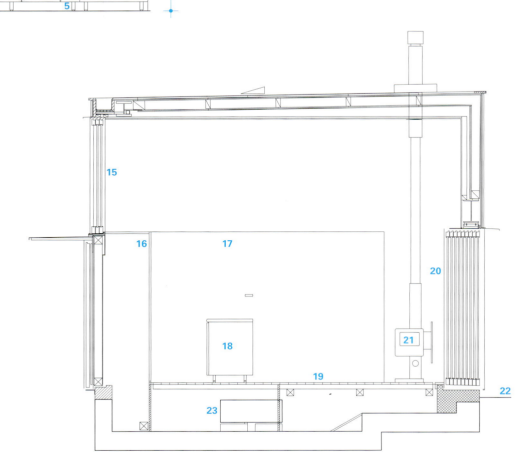

Materials
Worktop Stainless steel
Joinery Timber frame with stainless steel to island and timber veneer to full-height cupboards
Floor Tongue-and-groove pine flooring

Appliances and Fixtures
Taps and Spout Vola VL.KV1CDR-16
Sink Custom made, fully integrated stainless steel
Disposal Unit Insinkerator
Dishwasher Miele
Refrigerator Hoshizaki
Hob Fujimac
Oven Fujimac
Lighting Fluorescent fittings under elevated countertop

Project Credits
Completion 2003
Project Architects Takaharu Tezuka, Yui Tezuka, Masahiro Ikeda, Chie Nabeshima, Mayumi Miura
Structural Engineer Tezuka Architects + Masahiro Ikeda
Lighting Consultants Masahide Kakudate (Masahide Kakudate Lighting Architect & Associates, Inc.)
Main Contractor Nitadori Komuten

Simon Conder Associates

N1 Apartment
London, England, UK

The clients for this warehouse apartment in North London, a journalist and a photographer, wanted to create a spacious home on the second floor of a converted nineteenth-century industrial building. On a very tight budget, they were determined to make the most of the limited space, and in particular to retain and enhance the sense of space and light in the typically high-ceilinged, large-windowed shell.

As a result of their requirements, the space was not divided into separate rooms, but essentially left as a single open area. The rear wall of the space is lined with a white storage wall which accommodates the main services and the majority of the built-in storage. The

main focus of the space is a beautifully crafted timber box that cleverly accommodates the kitchen and bathroom. The box appears to float above the timber floor of the main space, and is accessed from the rear via steps to a raised platform.

Concealed lighting both in the recess where the box cantilevers out over the floor, and in the top, further reinforce the impression of lightness. A slot in the façade of the box facing the living space allows communication between the kitchen and guests, interrupted only by a stainless steel panel that acts as a screen to the hob.

The box also contains separate bath, shower and WC compartments which can be

used separately or, if the bath and WC doors are left in the open position, collectively to form a conventional bathroom.

The main space is divided into three areas by two mobile white storage units. The area adjacent to the bath compartment is used for sleeping and the area in front of the kitchen for living and dining, while the third area is used as a study.

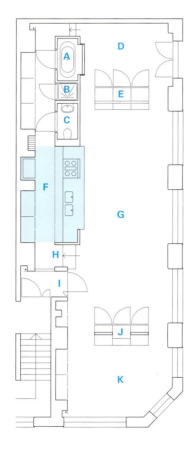

Opposite Left
View of the main living space, which is overlooked by the cantilevered timber box which in turn encloses a stainless steel kitchen and the bathroom. Plenty of natural light is admitted through the existing steel-framed warehouse windows, while the sense of uninterrupted space is enhanced by white mobile storage units.

Floor Plan
A Bathroom
B Shower room
C WC
D Bedroom
E Mobile storage unit
F Kitchen
G Living room
H Step up to kitchen galley
I Entrance
J Mobile storage unit
K Study

Left
The kitchen is made up of a series of stainless steel units. A slot is cut into the timber box to allow communication with the living space. Behind the kitchen bench is a full-height wall of storage and an integrated stainless steel fridge-freezer.

Steel

Simon Conder Associates
N1 Apartment
London, England, UK

Kitchen Plan and Elevation A
1:50
1 Gas hob
2 Line of timber ceiling
3 Stainless steel worktop
4 Stainless steel undermounted sink
5 Face of timber box to living room
6 Step up to kitchen from living room
7 Recessed stainless steel fridge-freezer
8 Recessed pantry cupboards
9 Opening to living room
10 Ductwork for extractor
11 Stainless steel extractor hood
12 Stainless steel backsplash
13 Stainless steel-clad MDF drawer and cupboard fronts
14 Oven
15 Spout and mixer tap
16 Integrated dishwasher

Detail Section A and Elevation B
1:10
1 Stainless steel worktop
2 MDF drawer interior
3 Adjustable MDF shelf
4 Adjustable plinth feet
5 Stainless steel facing to drawer front
6 Stainless steel facing to cupboard front
7 Stainless steel kickplate
8 Tongue-and-groove cladding
9 Timber framing with insulation to box wall
10 Concealed fluorescent lights
11 Tongue-and-groove floor boards to raised floor
12 Timber joists
13 Existing timber floor
14 Timber joists to support new floor
15 Timber kickplate

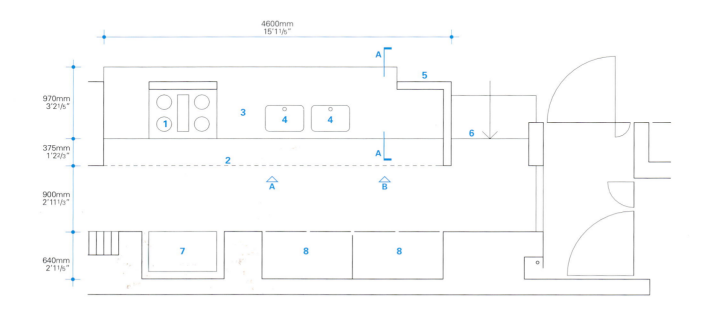

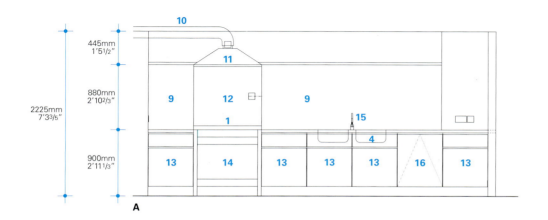

Materials
Worktop Stainless steel on two layers of 18 mm (3/4 inch) thick MDF
Joinery Typically stainless steel on 15 mm (3/5 inch) thick MDF
Floor Existing tongue-and-groove flooring to main space and new 19 mm (3/4 inch) thick tongue-and-groove to raised floor

Appliances and Fixtures
Taps Vola KV1 one-handle mixer with double swivel spout
Sink Stainless steel undermounted double sink
Dishwasher Supplied by client
Washing Machine Supplied by client
Refrigerator Supplied by client
Hob Smeg
Oven Smeg A1 Opera cooker in stainless steel
Extractor SMEG KSED95X chimney hood
Lighting Concealed fluorescent fittings above and below timber kitchen box

Project Credits
Completion 2000
Client Annalisa Barbieri and Pete Warren
Project Architects Simon Conder, Chris Neve
Main Contractor David Jones

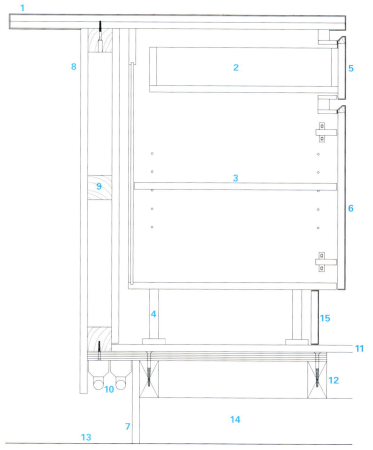

B

A–A

Ian Moore
Architects

Hay Barn
Mittagong, New South
Wales, Australia

This commission was originally for the refurbishment of an existing barn and cottage on a rural property along a ridge looking north towards a distant view. The cottage refurbishment formed the first stage of the project and consisted of extending an existing verandah around the southern face of the cottage, a new bathroom and kitchen and the addition of sun control louvres to the west-facing windows as well as a general tidy up and repainting.

Stage two was to have been the conversion of one half of an existing timber and corrugated iron barn into a studio space which could also double as occasional guest accommodation, while the other half was to retain its original use as a working barn and machinery shed. After inspection, however, it was determined that the original structure had deteriorated to such an extent that it was not viable to be retained. The decision was then taken to demolish the entire structure and build a totally new barn with an identical footprint, height and roof pitch to satisfy the local council.

The new structure consists of eight steel portal frames. The three western bays are utilized as the storage and machinery shed. The eastern three bays form the studio, living and dining areas while the central bay contains the bathroom, laundry and kitchen and the stair to the mezzanine containing a library and office space which can double as a bedroom. The north and east walls of the studio are extensively glazed with sliding glass doors to the lower portion and adjustable glass louvres to the upper half. All glazing is shaded by retractable adjustable aluminium louvres which, when closed, form a totally sealed silver box providing privacy and security as well as protection from the, at times, harsh climate.

Steel

Ian Moore Architects
Hay Barn
Mittagong, New South
Wales, Australia

Kitchen Plan
1:50
1 Stainless steel
  countertop
2 Stainless steel sunken
  countertop
3 Integral stainless
  steel sink
4 Mixer tap and spout
5 Line of dishwasher
  below

6 Line of oven below
7 Stainless steel gas hob
8 Line of refrigerator
  below
9 Full-height pantry store
  cupboard
10 Fridge-freezer concealed
   in cupboard
11 Laundry storage
12 Washer and dryer in
   cupboard

13 WC
14 Basin
15 Shower

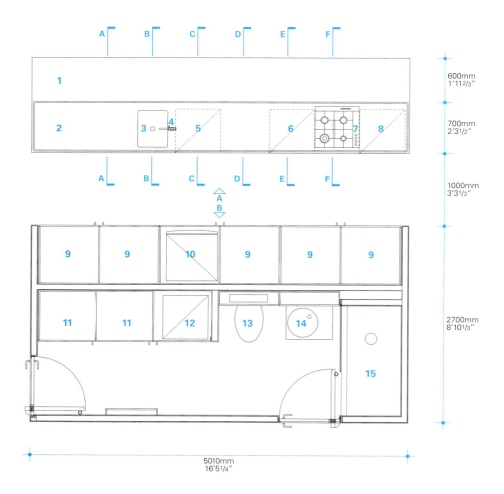

Kitchen
Elevations A and B
1:50
1 White laminate cupboard
  front
2 White laminate drawer
  fronts
3 Power outlets mounted
  on fixed laminate panel
4 Mixer tap and spout
5 Integral stainless steel

  sink
6 Waste bin
7 Integrated dishwasher
8 Stainless steel sunken
  countertop
9 Integrated oven
10 Stainless steel end panel
11 Stainless steel grille
   skirting
12 Adjustable shelving
   to pantry cupboard

13 Microwave oven
14 Power outlet
15 Fridge-freezer

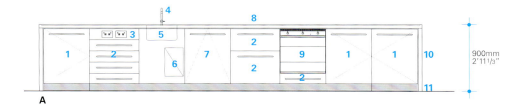

900mm
2'11 1/3"

A

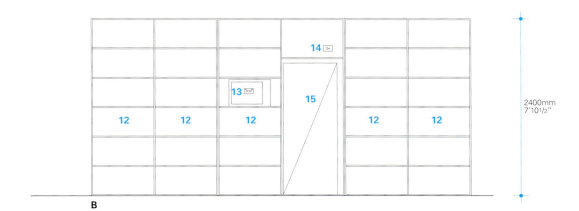

2400mm
7'10 1/2"

B

167

Steel

Ian Moore Architects
Hay Barn
Mittagong, New South
Wales, Australia

Unit Sections
1:20
1 Stainless steel
   countertop
2 Stainless steel sunken
   countertop
3 Integrated dishwasher
4 Fixed panel under bench
5 White laminate door
6 Stainless steel door pull
7 Stainless steel

grille plinth
8 Mixer tap and spout
9 Stainless steel sink
10 Adjustable shelf
11 White laminate cupboard
   door
12 Under-sink storage
13 Drawer
14 Integrated oven
15 White laminate pan
   drawer

16 Downdraft exhaust unit
17 Hob
18 Adjustable shelves to
   false-backed cupboard

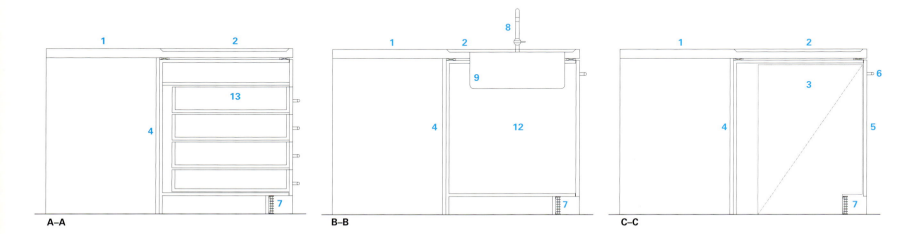

A–A   B–B   C–C

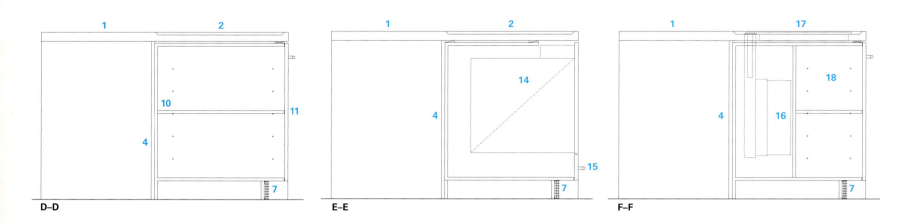

D–D   E–E   F–F

Materials
Worktop Stainless steel
Joinery White laminate
Floor Polished concrete slab
Tiles 100 x 100 mm (4 x 4 inch) gloss white ceramic tiles to bathroom floor

Appliances and Fixtures
Taps Vola
Spout Vola
Sink Integrated stainless steel
Dishwasher Smeg
Refrigerator Fisher and Paykel
Hob Smeg
Oven Smeg
Microwave Smeg
Extractor Smeg Pop Up Downdraft extractor
Lighting Erco spotlights and Kreon Diapason spotlights

Project Credits
Completion 2006
Client Trish and Ian Hay
Project Architects Ian Moore, Manuelle Schelp
Structural Engineers Peter Chan and Partners
Main Contractor Eastwick Country Homes
Landscape Architects Nicholas Bray Landscapes

Mark English Architects Sausalito Residence Sausalito, California, USA

The aim in designing this house was to create an elegant urban home with a warm modern ambiance. The interiors are comfortable and playful, and open up to the expansive view of San Francisco Bay. The site is a typical Sausalito hillside lot, small and sloping down from the street. To the north is a sweeping view of Sausalito, looking much like a town on the Amalfi Coast of Italy. To the east and south is an inspiring view of downtown San Francisco, across the Berkeley hills and Mount Diablo to Angel Island and Tiburon.

The existing three storey home was in a state of disrepair and was arranged as a series of small dark rooms connected by a convoluted staircase. The solution was to remove most of the interior walls through the use of structural steel, create a dramatic stair, and open the exterior walls to the views.

The kitchen is located on the middle level of the house and set back into the hillside beneath the parking deck with a mirrored back wall providing an expansive reflected view of San Francisco Bay. The layout of the kitchen is a simple U-shape with an island, open to the adjacent living and dining spaces. The centre island provides visual separation between the working and the entertaining areas, and is a feature in its own right.

The kitchen features ample counter space around the perimeter. The full-height cabinetry and tall appliances are hidden along one wall, eliminating the need for upper cabinets.

Finishes are in tune with the rest of the house. Kitchen cabinetry is custom designed and built using white, pre-catalyzed lacquer finish cabinets in combination with stainless-steel sheet metal and matching appliances. Black flamed granite countertops provide a lively texture at the work surfaces. Lighting plays an essential role creating a space where function and aesthetics coexist.

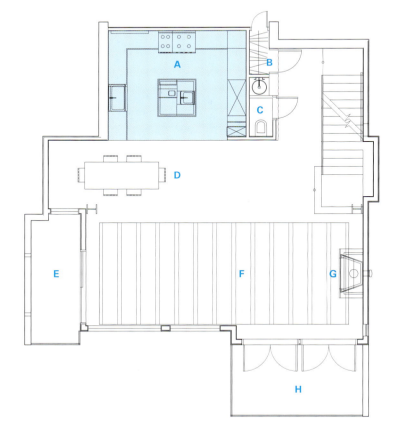

Opposite Left

The living, dining and kitchen areas are located on the middle level of this three storey house, which is arranged to relate to the steeply sloping site.

Floor Plan

A Kitchen
B Cloak room
C WC
D Dining room
E Terrace
F Living room
G Fireplace
H Terrace

Left

The kitchen is arranged in an L-shaped alcove with a stainless steel central island unit. Two runs of work space with open shelving above are complemented by a full wall of pantry storage and built-in fridge-freezer.

Bottom Left

The rear wall of the kitchen features a commercial grade gas hob and double oven with a mirrored splashback that reflects daylight from the full-height glazed doors opposite.

**Kitchen Plan and
Elevations A–C
1:50**
1 Base cabinet with drawer
   and cupboard
2 Sink with cabinet below
3 Dishwasher
4 Lazy Susan corner
   cabinet
5 Stainless utensil rods
6 Range cooker
7 Base cabinet
8 Microwave
9 Full-height cabinet with
   adjustable shelves
10 Refrigerator
11 Laundry shute
12 Phone niche in island
13 Trap to rubbish
   receptacle
14 Island prep sink
15 Wall-mounted mirror
16 Stainless steel shelf
17 Stainless steel tap
18 Side panel to base
   cabinet
19 Drawer cabinet
20 Range hood
21 Back guard to range
22 Black granite worktop
23 Drawer base cabinet
24 Sink cabinet
25 Wall-mounted glass
backsplash
26 Upper cabinet with door
27 Base cabinet
28 Full-height cabinet
29 Upper cabinet
30 Icemaker in refrigerator

**Island Elevations
D–G
1:50**
1 Stainless steel worktop
2 Drawer base cabinet
3 Base cabinet with door
4 Stainless steel tap
5 Fixed stainless steel
   panel
6 Pull-out rubbish bin
   cabinet
7 Stainless steel-lined
   phone niche

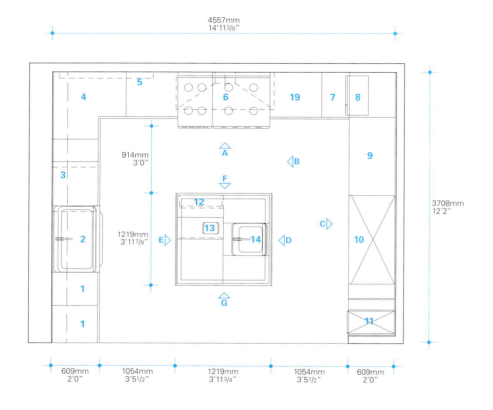

Materials
Worktop Perimeter kitchen in black flamed granite, island unit in stainless steel
Joinery Perimeter cabinets in white-painted finish (white pre-catalyzed lacquer finish by Mueller-Nicholls), island unit in stainless steel
Floor White oak planks, custom finished on site

Appliances and Fixtures
Taps and Spout Main tap by Blanco, island tap by Blanco
Sink Main sink Blanco stainless 512-751, Island prep sink by Blanco stainless 512-745, welded to stainless steel worktop
Disposal Unit Insinkerator
Dishwasher Bosch SHX56C05UC
Refrigerator Thermador KBUIT4850A
Range cooker Viking VDSC4876QSS
Microwave Amana AMC2206BAS stainless
Extractor Viking VCWH4848SS with Viking backguard
Lighting Lights over island by Bruck, Lighting Rainbow II

Project Credits
Completion 2007
Client Donna & Dennis Fecteau
Project Architects Mark English, Masha Barmina, Walter Evonuk
Structural Engineers Santos & Urrutia, Inc.
Joinery Mueller Nicholls
Lighting Consultant North Shore Consulting

B

C

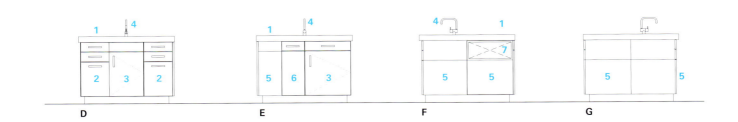

D   E   F   G

BAAS Jordi Badia / Mercé Sangenís, Architects

CH House
Barcelona, Spain

This vacation house is located in La Garriga near Barcelona, a town long associated with holidays thanks to its location between the plain of Vallès and the foothills of the Montseny mountains.

The longitudinal floor plan allows for access from both ends of the building, which is a response to the fact that the house sits on a sloping site between two streets. The principal entrance is on the upper street, while next to the lower one is the garage that, together with the swimming pool, bridges the slope and so creates a horizontal platform for the house and landscaped spaces that act as extensions of the domestic spaces within.

On one side of the house are ranged three children's or guest bedrooms, each with ensuite bathroom, and a study. The house is then bisected by the main entrance and a courtyard, on the other side of which the spaces are arranged as three parallel zones separated by walls of pale timber storage cupboards.

One of these spaces accommodates the master bedroom suite, complete with dressing room and large bathroom, while the central space contains the living room which is defined on one side by the stair up from the garage. On the other side of this wall are the dining room and kitchen, both of which have access to a generous west-facing terrace.

The kitchen consists of two main elements: a full height wall of timber-faced storage set against the stair wall, and a stainless steel island unit which sits alongside the dining table, but is separated from it by a glass wall. The island is complemented by a stainless steel slot in the timber wall that contains a sink and additional preparation space.

Floor Plan

A Guest bedroom and bathroom
B Guest bedroom and bathroom
C Guest bedroom and bathroom
D Study
E Courtyard
F Entrance
G Laundry
H Utility / store
I Dressing room
J Master bathroom
K Master bedroom
L Living room
M Terrace
N Stair from garage
O Cloak room
P WC
Q Kitchen
R Dining room

Left

View of the west terrace which is directly accessible from the dining room, living room and master bedroom.

Below Left

View of the kitchen from a glazed wall that offers views of the garden from both the kitchen and dining rooms.

Below Right

The kitchen consists of an island unit (right) and a wall of timber cupboards (left) that are separated from the dining area by a glass wall.

Steel

BAAS Jordi Badia / Mercé Sangenís, Architects
CH House
Barcelona, Spain

Kitchen Elevation A and Plan
1:50
1 Varnished beech veneer pantry cupboard door
2 Integrated refrigerator
3 Integrated freezer
4 Microwave
5 Oven
6 Varnished beech veneer drawers

7 Extractor hood in polished stainless steel
8 Chrome-plated mixer tap
9 Drawer unit
10 Stainless steel column
11 Island of varnished beech-veneer units wit stainless steel counter
12 Stainless steel splashback
13 Varnished beech-veneer

cupboards
14 Power outlet
15 Glass door with stainless steel frame
16 Santa and Cole Nova ceiling light
17 Dining table
18 Glass doors with stainless steel frame to terrace
19 Stainless steel worktop

20 Stainless steel sink
21 Gas hob
22 Limestone flooring

Section A–A
1:20
1 Adjustable shelves to pantry cupboard
2 Varnished beech-veneer pantry cupboard door
3 Limestone floor

4 Glass wall and door beyond
5 Extractor hood in polished stainless steel
6 Island of varnished beech veneer units with stainless steel counter
7 Steel column beyond
8 Glass doors to terrace
9 Roller blind

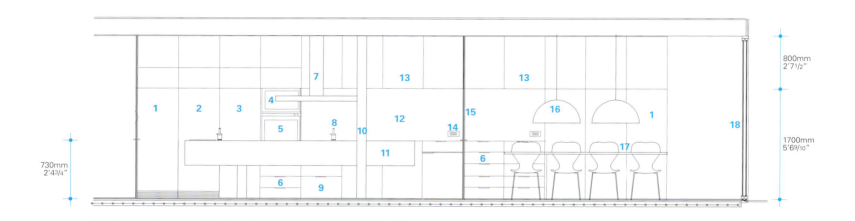

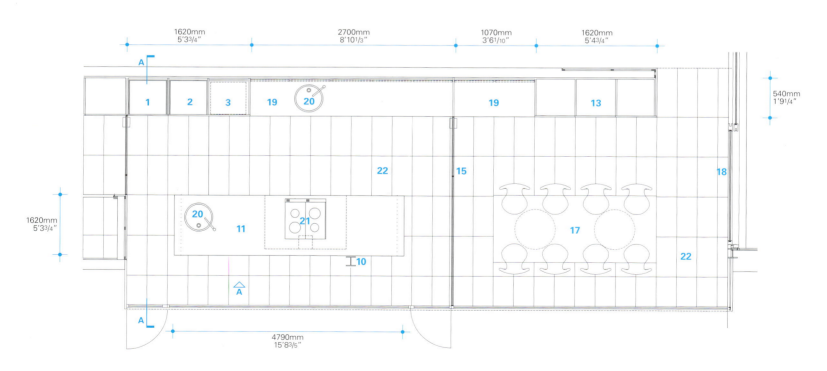

Materials
Worktop Stainless steel
Joinery Beech veneer
Floor 300 x 600 mm (12 x 24 inch) Cabra limestone

Appliances and Fixtures
Taps and Spout Hansgrohe Premium mixer tap and spout
Sink Integrated stainless steel Franke sink with Bulthaup waste disposal system
Refrigerator and Freezer Integrated side by side Liebre fridge-freezer Kle(v)2860 + GI 1983
Hob Digital Zanussi ceramic hob ZKT 662LX
Microwave Gaggenau EB 900
Extractor Gaggenau stainless steel AH180-190
Lighting Low voltage downlights to ceiling and Santa and Cole Nova ceiling light to dining room

Project Credits
Completion 2000
Project Architects Jordi Badia, Ignacio Forteza, Marcos Catalán (interior designer) Elena Valls, Tirma Balagué, Albert Cibiach, Rafael Berengena, Sergi Serrat
Structural Engineers Eduard Doce
Main Contractor Germans Pujol S.A

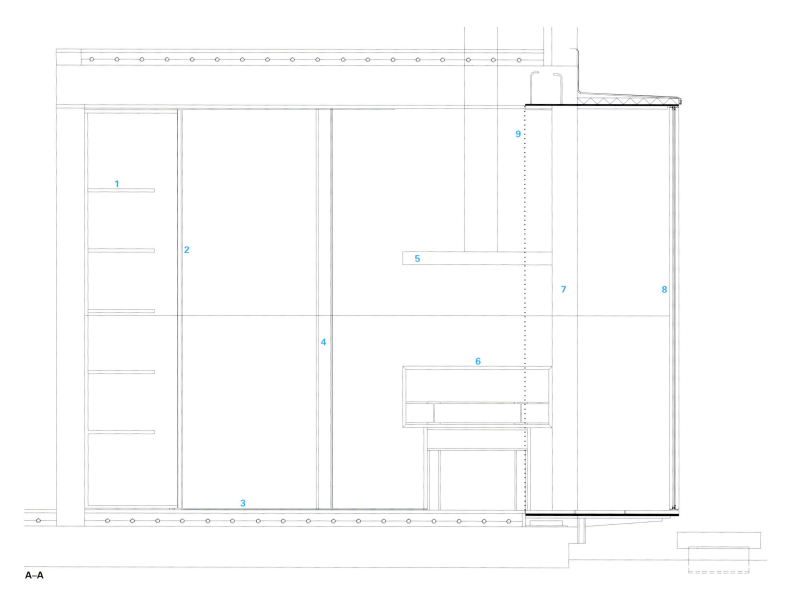

A–A

Johnny Grey with Haddow Partnership

The Threshing Barn
Hampshire, England, UK

This Grade Two listed building lay disused and in poor repair for many years, but the owner had a dream to turn it into a new house for their family designed to their own requirements. The planning process took two years to complete and work to retain and repair the original structure resulted in the majority of the original structure surviving – which adds to the unique character of the finished building.

In order to provide different spaces for the family to use independently, a full-height glass screen has been constructed between the family room and the other wing of the barn. In clear contrast to the old barn, all new work has been designed in a contemporary manner with simple lines and clear separation of new from old. Internally, crisp contemporary detailing contrasts with the original elements. Natural materials have been used throughout and where historic and contemporary elements meet, shadow gaps have been introduced to highlight the juxtaposition.

At the heart of the house is a sociable kitchen with views to the dining area, the gardens and a distant church tower. The kitchen features a circular counter with 360 degree views with raised serving bar. A tall, curved, double-sided cupboard is placed strategically across one segment of the circle to provide privacy from the front door. The geometry of storage furniture and appliances focussed on creating a relationship between the façades and the cooking circle.

A free-standing sink unit leaves the architecture visible and brings the washing up zone to the centre of room. The primary aim was to create easy flowing circulation and make the space feel comfortable to live in by using the traditional techniques of a furnished room. As a result, fitted furniture was avoided where possible, creating original but functional pieces that worked with the scale of the space.

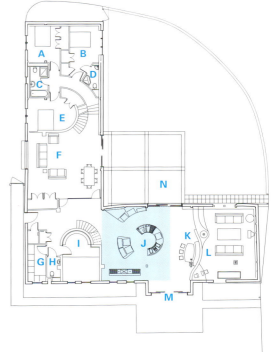

Opposite Left
The entrance to The Threshing Barn is via a double-height glazed opening in the west façade. From here it is possible to see through the barn to the kitchen and dining area to a paved east-facing terrace. A great deal of careful research was involved in conserving the historic building and in sympathetically matching new materials and finishes – including oak windows and thatched roof, seen here – with the old.

Floor Plan
A Bedroom
B Master bedroom
C Bathroom
D Master bathroom
E Guest bedroom
F Family room
G Utility room
H WC
I Library
J Kitchen
K Dining area
L Living room
M Entrance
N Terrace

Left
The kitchen is comprised of four separate elements which are designed as free-standing pieces of furniture that sit beneath the webbed canopy of the timber structure. The four elements are (from left to right), a prep bench with sink, a circular stainless steel cooking counter, a timber-clad fridge cabinet, and timber-clad pantry cupboards with integrated oven.

Below Left
View of the dining and living areas from the kitchen. Contemporary finishes such as large expanses of clear glazing, polished stone floors and stainless steel countertops contrast beautifully with the old structure.

**Kitchen Plan
1:50**
1 Draining board
2 Raised upstand to sinks
3 Stainless steel sink
4 Crockery compartment
5 Fridge-freezer
6 Walk-in pantry
7 Ovens
8 Appliance cupboard
9 Bakery
10 Domino hob
11 Wok hob
12 Stainless steel worktop
13 Oven
14 Chopping block
15 Raised glass bar

**Appliance Cupboard Plan
and Sections A–A, B–B and
C–C
1:50**
1 Walk-in pantry
2 Integrated ovens
3 Services void
4 Appliance cupboard
5 Sink
6 Baking cupboard
7 High-level storage
8 Timber veneer door
9 Storage cupboard
10 Appliance shelf
11 Timber kickplate
12 Warming drawers

**Refrigeration Unit Plan and
Sections A–A, B–B and C–C
1:50**
1 Integrated fridge-freezer
2 Storage drawers
3 Crockery storage
4 Timber veneer door to
  fridge-freezer
5 Glass canopy with
integrated lighting
6 Timber veneer door to
  crockery cupboard
7 Storage drawers
8 Glazed refrigerator
  doors
9 Timber kickplate
10 Refrigerator
11 Freezer
12 Stainless steel handle

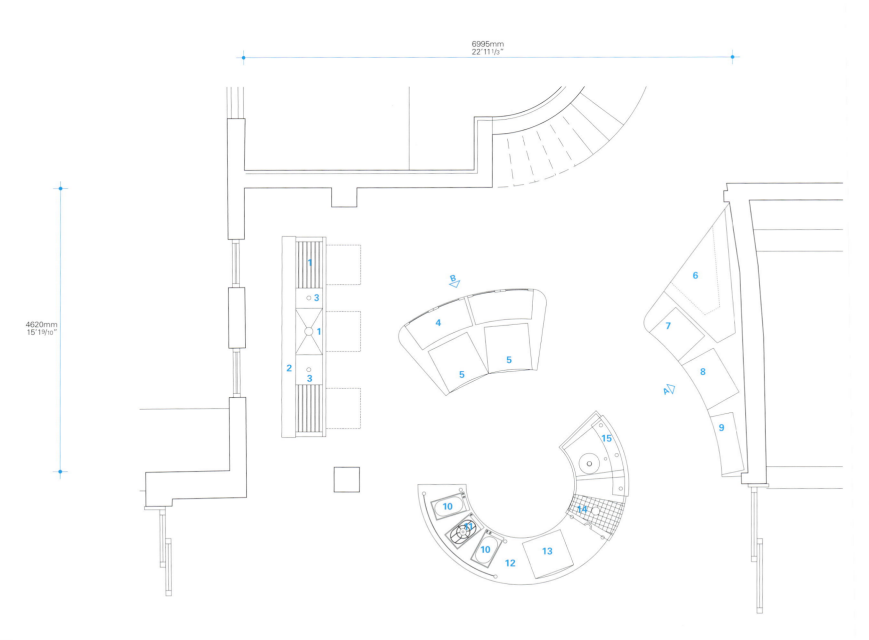

Materials
Worktop Honed Nero Zimbabwe Granite and brushed stainless steel
Joinery Sink tough in maple, teak and mazur birch, refrigerator and crockery cabinet in cherry and walnut, pantry in maple and walnut, island prep cabinet in ripple maple and maccasser ebony, island bench in birds eye maple with cherry slats
Floor Amtico within the cook zone

Appliances and Fixtures
Taps and Spout Cifial Techno 465 mixer taps in chrome
Sink Franke
Disposal Unit In-Sink-Erator
Dishwasher Fisher and Paykel
Refrigerator Siemens
Hob Siemens
Oven Siemens
Microwave Siemens

Project Credits
Completion 2006
Client Mr and Mrs R Naismith
Project Architects Johnny Grey, Robin Haddow, Bernadette Maguire, Miles Hartwell
Structural Engineers Stephen Penfold Associates
Quantity Surveyor Chris Newman Associates
Interior Design Johnny Grey Ltd
Lighting Consultant Deltalight

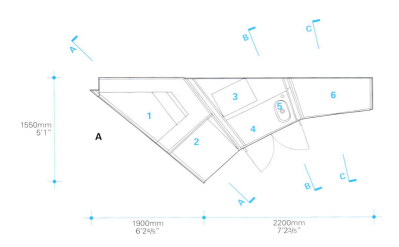

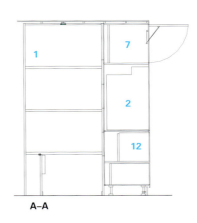

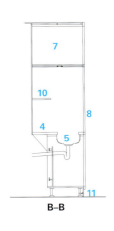

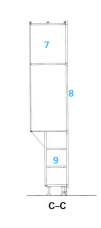

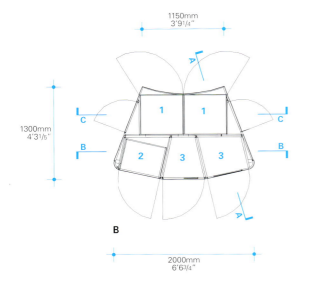

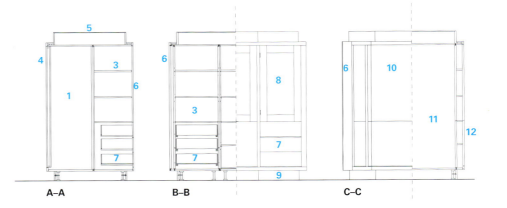

Fougeron Architecture

21 House
San Francisco,
California, USA

This remodel of a kitchen and bathroom in a Victorian home in San Francisco explores the effects of transparency in both the literal and material sense, and in the phenomenal sense. Exterior and interior glass walls allow light to create continuous, multiple readings of space at different points in time and with various interpretations.

The glass box is the perfect layer of protection between the communal nature of the kitchen and the private nature of the bathroom. This translucent wall speaks of sensuality and voyeurism. During the day, light is allowed into the bathroom from the south-facing kitchen, creating a bright, warm interior that accentuates the experience of bathing. In contrast, the translucent volume glows green at night through the use of jelled fluorescents, becoming a beacon for the gleaming kitchen. Old and new are integrated without obvious historical or stylistic references.

The historic order of this handsome Victorian house has been reinterpreted by creating alignments of circulation and emphasizing elements of the plan. Custom steel sections, doors and details for the exterior and interior glass walls convey the notion of craftsmanship and tectonics, linking old and new in a reciprocal dialogue.

The kitchen is arranged as a run of worktop with cupboards beneath along the solid flank wall of the house, which terminates at each end with tall storage units. A large freestanding stainless steel refrigerator, freezer and oven are located against the side wall.

An island bench stands in the centre of the room, providing extra preparation space as well as allowing the kitchen to function as a social space which is enhanced by its proximity to the garden. The palette throughout is kept to a minimum – white laminate for doors and drawers, and stainless steel for work surfaces and handles.

Opposite Left
Exterior view of the elegant bay-fronted, free-standing Victorian house.

Opposite Right
In the interior of the house, original features have been restored, giving the uncompromisingly contemporary kitchen and bathroom additions an historic context that adds meaning and drama to both old and new.

Floor Plan
A Stair up to entrance
B Entrance
C Living room
D Dining room
E Closet
F Guest bedroom
G Bathroom
H Kitchen
I Laundry
J Courtyard
K Stair up to garden

Left
View of the kitchen from the courtyard. Glazed doors open up the space to the garden.

Bottom Left
The countertop extends out on steel legs to create a place for the cook to sit and prepare food, or for family and friends to relax in the kitchen.

Bottom Right
The island bench is elevated on legs, allowing the floor finish to continue uninterrupted through the space. A translucent wall of glass separates the kitchen from the adjacent bathroom.

Steel

Fougeron Architecture

21 House
San Francisco, California,
USA

Kitchen Plan and Elevations
1:50

1 Bathroom
2 Laundry
3 Refrigerator
4 Cabinet with built-in oven
5 Pantry cupboard
6 Dishwasher under
7 Double stainless steel sink with disposal unit
8 Low cabinet
9 Appliance cabinet
10 Stainless steel top to island bench
11 Gas hob
12 Courtyard
13 Stair to garden
14 Storage
15 Freezer
16 Tall cabinet
17 Oven
18 Stainless steel drawers
19 Telephone outlet
20 Painted plasterboard wall
21 Side of tall cabinet
22 Tall unit with integrated fluorescent lighting to top of cabinet
23 Stainless steel splashback
24 Dishwasher
25 Stainless steel kickplate
26 Glass splashback
27 Stainless steel tap
28 Garbage disposal unit
29 White melamine drawer
30 White melamine cupboard
31 Insulated tempered glass panel
32 Steel-framed glass door to courtyard
33 Glass door to courtyard
(in section)
34 Steel-framed glass door to laundry
35 Translucent laminated safety glass partition wall

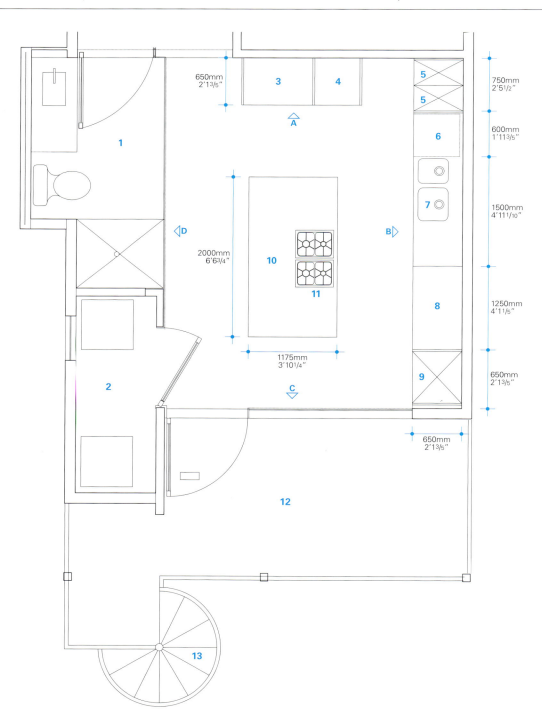

Materials
Worktop Plastic laminate and stainless steel to island
Joinery Plywood cabinetry by Bulthaup

Appliances and Fixtures
Spout KWC
Sink Stainless steel undermounted sink by Bulthaup
Disposal Unit Franke
Dishwasher Miele
Washing Machine Miele
Refrigerator Sub-Zero
Oven Gaggenau
Lighting Florescent T-5 fixtures above cabinetry, halogen recessed MR16 cans in ceiling

Project Credits
Completion 2003
Client Anne Fougeron
Project Architects Anne Fougeron, Russ Sherman, Michael Pierry, Todd Aranaz
Structural Engineers Endres Ware Engineers
Main Contractor Young & Burton

A

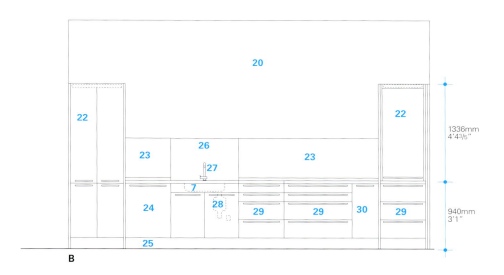

B

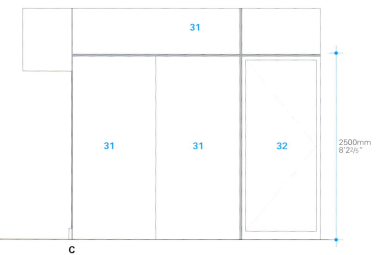

C

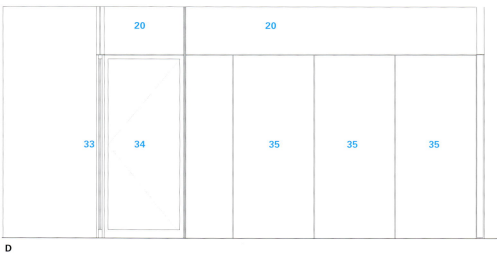

D

Crepain Binst Architecture

Loft
Antwerp, Belgium

This project for an office for up to 60 people as well as a private residence started life as a semi-derelict five-storey saddle-backed warehouse dating from c.1910. The building features beautiful cast-iron columns and vaulted brick arches in a handsome classical façade, all of which were restored to their former glory.

Despite the rather dilapidated state of the warehouse, the raw space had the potential to accommodate both the architect's office and his private residence. The building was rearranged to create a planted inner courtyard with parking spaces and central access to both the office and the apartment. In place of the former industrial lift, a single central black-lacquered concrete shaft was built to house a new lift, staircase and all of the electrical and hydraulic services.

Levels three and four accommodate the private residence with sleeping quarters, a multipurpose room and a workshop on the third floor and living spaces including kitchen and dining room above, all arranged around the west-facing roof terrace which offers panoramic views of the city from both the front and the back of the building.

The four metre (13 feet) high space allows the kitchen, ranged along one of the side walls, to be lit from above via a horizontal band of clear glazing. All of the main appliances – hob, oven, refrigerator – are located against the wall, where bench space also accommodates the sink and pantry storage.

An aluminium island bench features cantilevered ends for seating, and an elevated monolithic timber cutting board in the centre. Aluminium is used throughout, which perfectly complements both the industrial aesthetic of the original building and the rough cast concrete of the new walls.

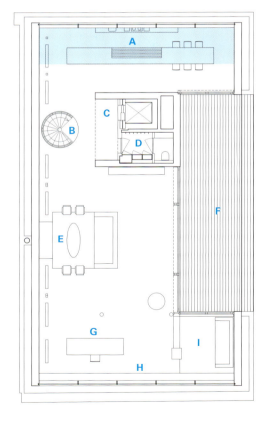

Opposite Left
View of the building from Antwerp Harbour. The renovated original brick façade (left centre) contrasts with new grey aluminium cladding to the apartment at the top of the building and the dark grey plaster to the office levels.

Floor Plan
A Kitchen
B Circular stair to lower level
C Entrance
D Cloak room
E Living room
F Terrace
G Study
H Library
I TV alcove

Left
View of the living room, study and library which, like the kitchen, features a band of high-level glazing. The apartment enjoys spectacular views of the city, including the spire of Antwerp Cathedral.

Below
The kitchen, constructed entirely from aluminium, includes space for dining in the shape of the extended island worktop. The central timber block is raised to an appropriate height for food preparation while standing.

Steel

Crepain Binst Architecture
Loft
Antwerp, Belgium

Kitchen Plan
1:50
1 Aluminium worktop
2 Integrated stainless steel sink
3 Wok burner
4 Gas hob
5 Grill
6 Cantilevered section of aluminium island bench
7 Raised timber chopping block to island bench
8 Cantilevered section of aluminium island bench / dining table
9 Glazed doors to terrace

Section A–A
Through Island
1:10
1 Raised timber chopping block to island bench
2 Aluminium sheet to island bench worktop
3 Aluminium box section
4 Aluminium side panel
5 Multi-ply structure to drawer
6 Aluminium L-section to kickplate
7 Aluminium-lined recessed pull handle
8 Aluminium sheet finger pull
9 Aluminium sheet to drawer front

Island Drawer Pull Detail
1:1
1 Aluminium sheet to island bench worktop
2 Aluminium box section
3 Aluminium sheet
4 Multi-ply substructure
5 Aluminium sheet finger pull
6 Multi-ply substructure to recessed pull handle
7 Aluminium sheet lining to recessed pull handle

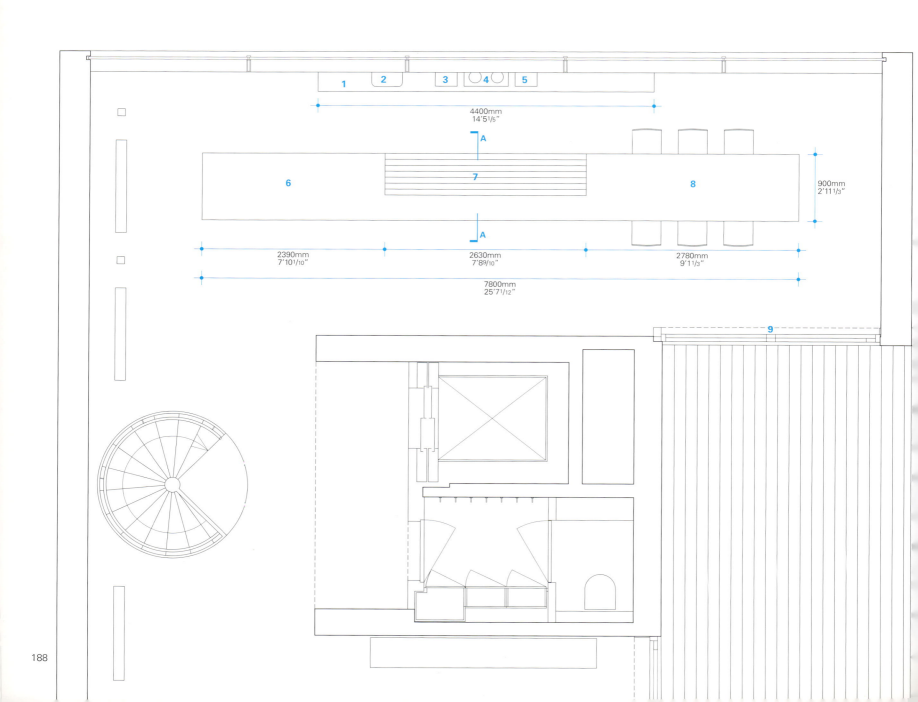

Materials
Worktop Stainless steel on the kitchen side and aluminium on the island bench
Joinery Aluminium sheets bonded to multi-ply timber
Floor Timber parquetry

Appliances and Fixtures
Taps Vola 590T36 design by Arne Jacobsen
Sink Integrated stainless steel sink
Dishwasher Integrated dishwasher by Küppersbush
Refrigerator Two integrated refrigerators by Küppersbush
Wok, Hob and Grill Integrated wok-system by Gaggenau
Oven Integrated oven by Smeg
Microwave Free-standing microwave by Siemens
Extractor Integrated extractor
Lighting Blue, red and green neon tube lights in floor and white neon tube lights above kitchen niche

Project Credits
Completion 1997
Client Crepain Family
Structural Engineer Archidee
Quantity Surveyor Steven de Paepe
Main Contractor Van Rymenant nv
Interior Designer Nadia Pelckmans

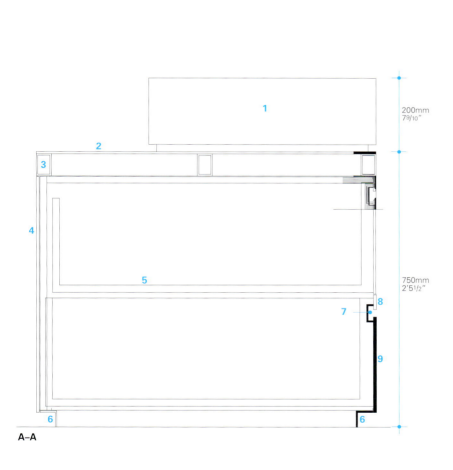

A–A

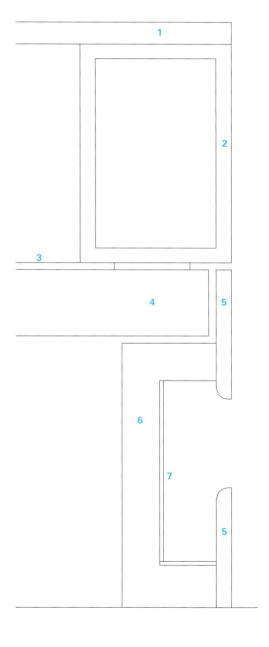

AUSTRALIA
Ian Moore Architects
44 McLachlan Avenue, Rushcutters Bay
Sydney, NSW 2011
T:+61 2 9380 4099 F:+61 9380 4302
info@ianmoorearchitects.com
www.ianmoorearchitects.com

Lippmann Associates
570 Crown Street, Surry Hills, NSW 2010
T:+61 2 9318 0844 F:+61 2 9319 2230
info@lippmann.com.au
www.lippmann.com.au

Marsh Cashman Koolloos Architects
Studio 401, 104 Commonwealth Street
Surry Hills, NSW 2010
T:+61 2 92114146 F:+61 2 92114148
architects@mckarchitects.com
www.mckarchitects.com

Tzannes Associates
63 Myrtle Street, Chippendale, NSW 2008
T:+61 2 9319 3744 F:+61 2 9698 1170
tzannes@tzannes.com.au
www.tzannes.com.au

Welsh + Major Architects
Level 1, 38 Waterloo Street
Surry Hills, NSW 2010
T:+61 2 9699 6066 F:+61 2 9699 6077
mail@welshmajor.com
www.welshmajor.com

BELGIUM
Architectenlab
Kempische Kaai 49, B 3500 Hasselt
and Ulensstraat 86 / 12, B 1080 Brussels
T:+32 11 87 25 82 F:+32 11 65 64 55
info@architectslab.com
www.architectslab.com

Crepain Binst Architecture
Vlaanderenstraat 6, B 2000 Antwerpen
T:+32 3 213 61 61 F:+32 3 213 61 62
mail@crepainbinst.be
www.crepainbinst.be

Vincent Van Duysen
Lombardenvest 34, B 2000 Antwerpen
T:+32 3 205 91 90
vincent@vincentvanduysen.com
www.vincentvanduysen.com

FINLAND
Huttunen-Lipasti Architects
Hietalahdenkatu 9B T3, 00180 Helsinki
T:+358 9 6947724 F:+358 9 6947724
mail@huttunen-lipasti.fi
www.huttunen-lipasti.f

IRELAND
Donaghy + Dimond Architects
41 Francis Street, Dublin 8
T:+353 1 416 8132 F:+353 1 416 9730
info@donaghydimond.ie
www.donaghydimond.ie

JAPAN
EDH Endoh Design House
#101, 2-13-8, Honmachi
Shibuya-ku, Tokyo 151-0071
T:+81 (0) 3-3377-6293
endoh@edh-web.com
www.edh-web.com

Tezuka Architects + Masahiro Ikeda
1-19-9-3F Todoroki Setagaya
Tokyo 158-0082
T:+81 3 3703 7056 F:+81 3 3703 7038
tez@sepia.ocn.ne.jp
www.tezuka-arch.com

NEW ZEALAND
Morgan Cronin
PO Box 28-700, Remuera, Auckland
T:+64 09 813 6192 F:+64 09 813 6299
info@croninkitchens.co.nz
www.croninkitchens.co.nz

SPAIN
**BAAS Jordi Badia / Mercé Sangenís,
Architects**
Frederic Rahola 63, Baixos Local 1
08032 Barcelona
T:+34 93 358 01 11 F:+34 93 358 01 94
baas@jordibadia.com
www.jordibadia.com

**Pablo Fernàndez Lorenzo and Pablo
Redondo Diez Architects**
Primavera 9, 4° exterior derecha
Madrid 28012
9796pablofl@coam.es

UK
Claridge Architects
Unit 11, The Tay Building
2A Wrentham Avenue, London, NW10 3HA
T:+44 20 8969 9223 F:+44 20 8969 9224
info@claridgearchitects.com
www.claridgedesign.com

Haddow Partnership
Market Place House, 2-4 Market Place,
Basingstoke, Hants, RG21 7QA
T:+44 1256 335000 F:+44 1256 472385
info@haddowpartnership.co.uk
www.haddowpartnership.co.uk

Hudson Architects
49-59 Old Street, London, ECIV 9HX
T:+44 20 7490 3411 F:+44 20 7490 3412
info@hudsonarchitects.co.uk
www.hudsonarchitects.co.uk

Jamie Fobert Architects
5 Crescent Row, London, EC1Y 0SP
T:+44 207 553 6563 F:+44 207 553 6566
mail@jamiefobertarchitects.com
www.jamiefobertarchitects.com

Niall McLaughlin Architects
39–51 Highgate Road, London, NW5 1RS
T:+44 20 7485 9170 F:+44 20 7485 9171
info@niallmclaughlin.com
www.niallmclaughlin.com

John Pawson
Unit B 70-78 York Way, London, N1 9AG
T:+44 20 7837 2929 F:+44 20 7837 4949
email@johnpawson.com
www.johnpawson.com

Johnny Grey
Fyning Copse, Fyning Lane
Rogate, Hampshire, GU31 5DH
T:+44 1730 821 424
info@johnnygrey.co.uk
www.johnnygrey.co.uk

Levitate Architecture and Design Studio
161 Rosebery Avenue, London, EC1R 4QX
T: +44 20 7833 4455 F: +44 20 7833 4500
studio@levitate.uk.com
www.levitate.uk.com

Scape Architects
Unit 2, Providence Yard, London E2 7RJ
T:+44 20 7012 1244 F:+44 20 7012 1255
mail@scape-architects.com
www.scape-architects.com

Simon Conder Associates
Nile Street Studios, 8 Nile Street,
London, N1 7RF
T:+44 20 7251 2144 F:+44 20 7251 2145
sca@simonconder.co.uk
www.simonconder.co.uk

Turner Castle Architects
22 Iliffe Yard, Crampton Street,
London, SE17 3QA
T:+44 20 7431 2507
office@turnercastle.co.uk
www.turnercastle.co.uk

Westarchitecture
Bridge Studios, Hammersmith Bridge
London, W6 9DA
+44 794 181 4114 F:+1 415 362 9104
graham@westarchitecture.co.uk

USA
Barton Myers Associates
1025 Westwood Boulevard
Los Angeles, CA 90024
T:+1 310 208 2227 F:+1 310 208 2207
p_robertson@bartonmyers.com
www.bartonmyers.com

CCS Architecture
44 McLea Court, San Francisco, CA 94103
T:+1 415 864 2800 F:+1 415 864 2850
info@ccs-architecture.com
www.ccs-architecture.com
180 Varick Street, No.902 New York, NY 10014
T:+1 212 274 1121 F:+1 212 274 1122

Fougeron Architecture
431 Tehama Street, Suite 1
San Francisco, CA 94103
T:+1 415 641 5744 F:+1 415 282 6434
anne@fougeron.com
www.fougeron.com

Kaehler Moore Architects
A: 80 Greenwich Avenue
Greenwich, CT 06830
T:+1 203 629 2212 F:+1 203 629 0717
lek@kaehler-moore.com
www.kaehler-moore.com

Mark English Architects
250 Columbus Avenue, Suite 200
San Francisco, CA 94133
T:+1 415 391 0186 F:+1 415 362 9104
info@markenglisharchitects.com
www.markenglisharchitects.com

Resources

The following are internet addresses for sourcing fittings and appliances featured throughout the book. Unless otherwise indicated, these are international manufacturers and suppliers.

Abbey Kitchens
www.abbeykitchens.co.uk (Europe)

Abode
www.sinksandtaps.com (UK supplier)

AEG
www.aeg-electrolux.com

Agabekov
www.agabekov.com

Amana
www.amana.co.uk (UK)
www.amana.com (US)

Amtico
www.amtico.com

Artek
www.artek.fi

Asko
www.asko.se

B+W
www.bowers-wilkins.com

BBS Timber
www.bbstimbers.co.nz (ANZ)

Beechway Joinery
www.beechwayjoinery.co.uk (UK)

Binova
www.binova.com

Blanco
www.blanco.com

Bosch
www.bosch.com

Britannia
www.britannialiving.co.uk (UK)

Broan-Nu Tone
www.broan.com (US / CAN)

Bruck
www.brucklightingsystems.com (US)

Bulthaup
www.bulthaup.com

Capri
www.caprilighting.com (US)

Chicago
www.chicagofaucets.com (US)

Cifial
www.cifial.co.uk (UK)

Corian
www.corian.com

Dacor
www.dacor.com (US)

De Deitrich
www.dedietrich.co.uk

Deltalight
www.deltalight.com

Dornbracht
www.dornbracht.com

Electrolux
www.electrolux.com

Elica DR
www.elica.com

Endo
www.endo-lighting.com

Fagerhult
www.fagerhult.com

Farrar Stone
www.farrar.co.uk (UK)

Fisher and Paykel
www.fisherpaykel.com

Franke
www.franke.com

Gaggenau
www.gaggenau.com

Habitat
www.habitat.net

Hafele
www.hafele.com

Hansgrohe
www.hansgrohe.com

Hera
www.hera-online.com

Hoshizaki
www.hoshizaki.com

Iguzzini
www.iguzzini.com

InSinkErator
www.insinkerator.com

Jenn-Air
www.jennair.com (US)

Kohler
www.kohler.com

Kreon
www.kreon.com

Kuppersbusch
www.kueppersbusch.de

KWC
www.kwc.com

Liebherr
www.liebherr.com

Louis Poulsen
www.louispoulsen.com

Lutron Electricals
www.lutron.com

Maytag
www.maytag.co.uk (UK)
www.maytag.com (US)

MGS Boma
www.mgsprogetti.com

Miele
www.miele.co.uk (UK)
www.miele.com (US)

Mitsubishi Electric
www.mitsubishielectric.com

MK
www.mkelectric.co.uk

Mueller Nicholls
www.mnbuild.com (US)

Novy
www.novy.com

Panasonic
www.panasonic.net

Philips
www.philips.com

Qasair
www.qasair.com.au (AUS/Asia)

Roger Seller Nostromo
www.rogerseller.com.au (AUS)

Sharp
www.sharp.co.uk (UK)
www.sharpusa.com (US)

Siemens
www.siemens.com

SKK
www.skk.net

Skope
www.skope.co.uk (Europe)

Smeg
www.smeg.com

Stala
www.stala.com (Europe)

Sub-Zero
www.subzero.com

Targetti Squadra
www.targetti.com

Tekna
www.tekna.be

Thermador
www.thermador.com (US)

Venduro
www.venduro.be

Viking
www.vikingrange.com

Vola
www.vola.com

Zanussi
www.electrolux.com

Picture Credits

All architectural drawings are
supplied courtesy of the architects

Photographic credits:
7   © Dennis Gilbert / VIEW
11 © Peter Cook / VIEW
13 © Peter Cook / VIEW
15 Courtesy Welsh + Major Architects
17 Courtesy Welsh + Major Architects
19 © Keith Collie
21 © Keith Collie
24 © Giorgio Possenti
25 © Koen van Damme
30 Philippe van Gelooven
31 Philippe van Gelooven (left)
31 Anja van Eetveldt (right)
34 © Keith Collie
35 © Keith Collie
37 © Keith Collie
38 Toon Grobet / www.toongrobet.be
39 Toon Grobet / www.toongrobet.be
43 Toon Grobet / www.toongrobet.be
    (centre, bottom right)
43 Mich Verbelen (bottom left)
44 © Edmund Sumner / VIEW
45 © Edmund Sumner / VIEW
49 © Edmund Sumner / VIEW
50 © Willem Rethmeier
51 © Willem Rethmeier
55 © Willem Rethmeier
56 © Peter Cook / VIEW
57 © Peter Cook / VIEW
61 © Peter Cook / VIEW
62 © Ciro Coelho / www.cirocoelho.com
63 © Ciro Coelho / www.cirocoelho.com
66 Steve Townsend /
    www.stownsend.com
67 Steve Townsend /
    www.stownsend.com
74 © Kraig Carlstrom
75 © Kraig Carlstrom
79 © Kraig Carlstrom
80 © Sue Barr
81 © Sue Barr
84 Kai Fagerström
85 Mika Vuoto
89 Mika Vuoto
90 © Willem Rethmeier
91 © Willem Rethmeier
94 © Nick Kane
95 © Nick Kane (top)
95 Courtesy Niall McLaughlin Architects
    (bottom)
100 © Kilian O'Sullivan
101 © Kilian O'Sullivan
105 © Kilian O'Sullivan
106 © Keith Collie
107 © Keith Collie

111 © Keith Collie
112 Eric Laignel
113 Eric Laignel
116 Hiroyasu Sakaguchi
117 Hiroyasu Sakaguchi
120 © Philip Lauterbach / www.plpix.com
121 © Dennis Gilbert / VIEW
125 © Dennis Gilbert / VIEW
126 Inés Sagastume / Eugeni Pons
127 Inés Sagastume / Eugeni Pons
130 Mark LaMonica Photography /
    www.lamonicapictures.com
131 Mark LaMonica Photography /
    www.lamonicapictures.com
134 © Peter Cook / VIEW
135 © Peter Cook / VIEW
138 Kallan MacLeod /
    www.KallanMacLeod.com
139 Kallan MacLeod /
    www.KallanMacLeod.com
144 John Gollings
145 John Gollings
149 John Gollings
150 © Richard Glover / VIEW
151 © Richard Glover / VIEW (top left
    and right)
151 Max Creasy (centre left)
156 Katsuhisa Kida
157 Katsuhisa Kida
159 Katsuhisa Kida
160 Peter Warren /
    www.peterwarren.co.uk
161 Peter Warren /
    www.peterwarren.co.uk
164 Ross Honeysett
165 Ross Honeysett
169 Ross Honeysett
170 Claudio Santini
171 Claudio Santini
175 Eugeni Pons
178 Courtesy Haddow Partnership
179 Courtesy Haddow Partnership
182 Matthew Millman
183 Matthew Millman
186 Ludo Noël
187 Toon Grobet / www.toongrobet.be

Acknowledgments

Thanks above all to the architects who
submitted material for this book. Their time,
effort and patience is very much appreciated.
Special thanks to Hamish Muir and Sophia
Gibb for the design and picture research
respectively. Thanks also to Philip Cooper and
Gaynor Sermon at Laurence King and to
Justin Fletcher for editing the drawings. And
finally a special thanks to my husband
Vishwa Kaushal.